MAN AS SYMPHONY
OF THE CREATIVE WORD

RUDOLF STEINER

MAN AS SYMPHONY OF THE CREATIVE WORD

Twelve Lectures given in Dornach, Switzerland
from October 19th to November 11th, 1923

Translated by

Judith Compton-Burnett

RUDOLF STEINER PRESS, LONDON

First published in English by Rudolf Steiner Publishing Co. London (no date)

Second Edition by Rudolf Steiner Publishing Co. London and Anthroposophic Press, New York, 1945

Third Edition (new translation) by Rudolf Steiner Press, London, 1970
Reprinted (paperback only) 1978

Translated from shorthand reports unrevised by the lecturer

The German text is published under the title *Der Mensch als Zusammenklang des schaffenden, bildenden und gestaltenden Weltenwortes* (Bibl. No. 230)

This English edition is published in agreement with the *Rudolf Steiner Nachlassverwaltung*, Dornach, Switzerland

ISBN 0 85440 324 8

Printed and bound in Great Britain at
The Camelot Press Ltd, Southampton

CONTENTS

SYNOPSIS

Lecture III

Physical and spiritual substance. In the lower organization of man (limbs) spiritual substance predominates, in the upper (head) physical. Distinction between substance and forces. In the head, forces are spiritual, in limb system, physical. Use of this knowledge in healing. Man's two-fold debt to the earth in that he takes into death spiritual substance (of limbs) which the earth needs, and leaves behind physical substance (of head) which he has estranged from the earth. Hence arises imbalance and suffering of the earth to be rectified in future planetary epochs. But what man is at present unable to do is performed by the eagle (type of the birds) and the cow (type of the essential animal). Through its feathers the eagle carries spiritualized earth substance into the spiritual world: through its digestive processes the cow gives materialized spirit substance to the earth. Initiation Science lives in the feelings aroused by such knowledge. Rejoicing of earth-spirits in the activities of the cow, and of air and fire spirits in activities of the eagle. Criticism of a sequel to Albert Schweitzer's earlier book. The lion as organizing the right balance between eagle and cow.

PART TWO

Lecture IV

Recapitulation of the four stages of Earth Evolution: Saturn (Warmth), Sun (Air), Moon (Water), Earth (Solid). Distinction between the upper nature of the first two, and the lower nature of the second two. Each stage of evolution leaves its effects in later stages, e.g. Moon forces left in the earth work in magnetism and gravity. The butterfly is a creation of the upper cosmic forces. Its egg is under direct influence of the sun, the caterpillar of Mars, the chrysalis of Jupiter, and the freed butterfly of the light permeated by Saturn. In the Moon evolution the plant germs separated and came under the influence of lower forces. The plant seed belongs to the earth; the leaf corresponds to the crawling caterpillar; the calyx to the cocoon; the flower to the freed butterfly. Influences of the lower planets—Moon, Venus, Mercury—supplant the upper planets which influence the butterfly. The butterfly is the freed plant, the plant the fettered butterfly. Their joy in each other. Artistic perception needed for true knowledge.

Lecture V

Recapitulation. The butterfly continually gives spiritualized substance to the cosmos during life, not only, like the birds, at death. Butterflies are creatures of light-ether, birds of warmth. How warmed air penetrates bones, etc. of birds. A bird's physical body is merely its "luggage". How the butterfly takes light-filled air into its body. Both bird and butterfly overcome gravity, while bats are subject to it. They dislike light, and their flight is mechanical. Butterflies see earth as mirror of cosmos, birds see what lives in air, bats begin to perceive things of earth but are full of listening fear. Butterflies are memories, birds are thoughts, bats are dreams. Bats also give off spiritualized substance but impart it to the atmosphere, as a kind of "magma" in the air. People were once taught to defend themselves against this which, when breathed by man, becomes the nutriment of the Dragon. The Michael impulse protects man today.

Lecture VI

Man has the longest evolution, beginning with the head on Saturn, when butterflies also appeared. Man develops inwardly, the butterfly outwardly. Breast-system appears on Sun with the lion, which added head and limbs later. Digestive system appears on Moon with the cow, which added breast and head. Amphibians and reptiles are purely digestion animals. Fish appear when man develops reproductive organs. Butterflies and birds are a metamorphosed memory, in miniature, of the Beings of the Hierarchies man knew on Saturn and Sun. Hence they are rightly used as pictures of spiritual beings. On descending to a new incarnation man first encounters the butterfly "corona" shot through with rays from birds, i.e. the head nature. Fishes do not feel themselves as water-beings, but as beings enveloping

water—as etheric creatures. They are aware of the
"breathing" of the earth. The frog is connected with the
astral of the earth, and responds to weather conditions. The
Cosmos creates frogs, toads, snakes, etc. through same forces
as digestion. Relation of toads to large intestine. Study of the
mineral kingdom will reveal the future as study of animals
has revealed the past. Formation of minerals. The pineal
gland.

PART THREE

Lecture VII

Mystery of plant life. Gnomes, which work in roots, are
sense organs in which perceiving and comprehending are
one. They despise human logic. Through the plant they
gaze at the forces of the universe while remaining connected
with the earth. The earth threatens them with the danger of
becoming frogs or toads. Undines or water-spirits work in
leaf formation, living in the moist air. They dream the
chemistry of plant life. Their fear is to become fish. Sylphs
live in warm air, especially in air movement caused by
birds, which give them a feeling of ego. They bear cosmic
love through the atmosphere, and are light-bearers, weaving
archetypal plant forms out of light, which later fall down to
the gnomes. Salamanders or fire spirits live in light-warmth
which they carry to the blossoms in the pollen, which in
turn the stamens carry to the seed-bud. All this is a male
process. Fructification takes place in winter when seeds meet
the ideal plant forms received by the gnomes. Goethe's
instinctive feeling for this. Fire spirits feel their ego in
connection with insects which actually live in their aura.
Hence comes the power of butterflies to spiritualise matter.
Gnomes and undines bear gravity forces of earth upwards to
meet light and warmth sent down by sylphs and salamanders.
Wonder of nature enhanced by spiritual science.

Lecture VIII

Ancient powers of spiritual perception have withdrawn.
Late evolved creatures, corresponding to head evolution in

man, lack a bone system and are spiritually completed by gnomes. Gnomes form their bodies out of gravity. The acuteness of their attention to the world. They are masked behind our dreams. Undines support animals requiring a bony covering. They are hidden behind our dreamless sleep. Sylphs supply the limb-system to birds. They lie behind man's waking dreams. Fire spirits complete butterflies in their bodily nature. The butterfly, with its fire spirit, resembles a winged man. Fire beings stand behind waking consciousness and thoughts. Malicious gnomes and undines produce parasites. Relation of excretion to the brain. Malicious sylphs produce poisons, e.g. bella donna. Fire spirits and poisonous almonds. Brahma, Vishnu, Shiva.

Lecture IX

For the gnomes solid earth is hollow and offers no resistance. They experience the different qualities of its substances. Their relation to the moon, and their different appearance at its phases. Their work in carrying over the hard structure from one manifestation to another. Undines and sylphs find their true life in death. Undines assimilate the colours of phosphorescent water, and offer themselves to the hierarchies. The sylphs carry the astrality of dying birds to the hierarchies. The fire beings do the same with the gleaming of the warmth ether on the butterflies' wings. All four classes of elemental beings are astonished at man's lack of awareness in sleep. They speak to man in admonishment. Their sayings, which form part of the creative Word.

PART FOUR

Lecture X

Origin of the different systems of man. Limb system from the Earth, Metabolic system from the Moon, Rhythmic system from the Sun, Nerve-senses system from Saturn. All substances taken into the body must be transformed: Mineral into Warmth ether, Plant into Air processes, Animal into Water processes. Only the pure human may be saved. Carbon created in man disperses ether, which penetrates sense organs and opens man to spiritual influences. Metabolic processes would cause illness, if they were not kept in check by healing processes born on Sun. Breathing has a cosmic rhythm and restrains the circulation rhythm. Comparison with Saturn. Joy of the first two hierarchies in this healing process. Man's spiritual activity in relation to healing. Inflammation caused by blood processes entering nerves: swellings and growths, by nerve processes entering the blood. Relation of education to health. World healing processes in the function of metals. Human therapy a microcosm of world therapy.

Lecture XI

All food must be transformed in the human organism. Mineral substance must be turned to warmth ether to receive cosmic forces for the building of the body. Children can only transform milk. Untransformed substances cause disease, e.g. diabetes. External warmth also must not enter the body. What root and flower in the plant say to man. Roots laid down when moon was united with the earth. The plant was liberated when the moon left the earth. Earthbound root and heaven-striving flower reverse their position when the plant becomes an air-being in man. In digestion pod-bearing plants (e.g. beans) do not reach the head. The reversal of the plant cannot properly take place in animal digestion. Elemental spirits of fear counter the animal's satisfaction in digestion. Kamaloka of carnivorous animals. Anthroposophy never fanatical (e.g. in diet) but only shows the truth. Milk working in the head for young children has its counterpart for old people in honey, the beestock being a head without a skull in outer nature. "A land flowing with milk and honey."

Lecture XII

The spiritual-moral has become convention today. Its real source is human understanding and love. Why do we see the opposite in actual life? Hatred and misunderstanding spring not from the spiritual but from the physical. The relation of the bone in man to hatred, and of the blood to misunderstanding and moral coldness. Terror in initiation in perceiving that the body is built of hatred and coldness, which always live in our sub-conscious. We take the coldness and hatred, learnt from the body into the spiritual world at death, where they are taken from us by the third and second hierarchies. This enables us to meet the first hierarchy at the "midnight hour". Here man's form dissolves from head downward, and a new spiritual form created which becomes the head of the future man. Thinking with the limbs. Rhythmic and digestive organs by the second and third hierarchies. Hatred necessary for structure of bones. Today hatred and coldness not fully absorbed by human beings and enter civilization as a cancer. The antidote to this cancer is Waldorf education.

Part One

Man as Symphony of the Creative Word

The Connection between Cosmic Conditions, Earthly Conditions, the Animal World and Man

You cannot deal with man through logic alone, but through an understanding that can only be reached when intellect shall see the world as a work of art.

LECTURE I

19th October, 1923

It has often been said in our studies, as was also evident in the recent lectures on the cycle of the year and the Michael problem, that man in his whole structure, in the conditions of his life, indeed in all that he is, presents a Little World, a Microcosm over against the Macrocosm : that he actually contains within himself all the laws, all the secrets, of the world. You must not, however, suppose that a full under-standing of this quite abstract sentence is a simple matter. You must penetrate into the manifold secrets of the world in order to find these secrets again in man.

Today we will consider this subject along certain lines of approach. We will examine first the world, and then man, in order to find how the human being exists as a Little World within the Great World. Naturally, what can be said about the Great World can never be more than fragmentary. It can never present anything complete in itself; for then our studies would have to traverse the whole world !

Let us first turn our attention to that realm which repre-sents what is immediately above man—the birds, which live essentially in the air.

It certainly cannot escape us that the birds which live in the air, creating the conditions of their existence out of the air, are formed differently from the animals which live either on the actual surface of the earth, or below it. When we consider the kingdom of the birds, we shall naturally find, in accordance with the generally accepted views, that in their case, as with other animals, we must speak of head, limb-system, and so on. But this is a thoroughly inartistic way of looking at things. I have often drawn attention to the fact that, if we are really to understand the world, we cannot remain at the stage of mere intellectual comprehension, but that what is intellectual must gradually change into an artistic conception of the world. Then you will certainly not be able to regard the head of a bird—so dwarfed and stunted in its form when compared to the head in other animals—as a head in the true sense. Certainly from the external, intellectual point of view one can say : The bird has a head, a body, and limbs. But just consider how stunted are the legs of a bird in comparison, let us say, with those of a camel or an elephant, and how dwarfed its head when compared with that of a lion or a dog. There is really hardly anything to speak of in a bird's head; there is hardly more to it than what in a dog or an elephant or a cat, is to be found in the front part of the mouth. I could put it in this way : it is the slightly more complicated front part of a mammal's mouth which corresponds to the head of a bird. And the limb-system in a mammal is completely stunted in the case of a bird. Certainly, an inartistic method of observation does speak about the fore-limbs of a bird as being metamorphosed into wings. But all this is thoroughly inartistic, unimaginative observation. If we would really understand nature, really penetrate into the cosmos, we must consider things in a deeper way—and this most especially in regard to their formative and creative forces. The view that the bird, too, simply has a head, a body and limbs can never lead to a true understanding of a bird's etheric body. For if, through imaginative contemplation, we advance from seeing what is physical in the bird to seeing what is etheric, then in the etheric bird there is only a head. When looking at the etheric bird one immediately comprehends that the bird allows of no comparison with the head, body and limbs of other animals, but must be regarded simply and solely as head, as metamorphosed head. So that the actual bird-head presents only the palate and front parts of the head, in fact the mouth; and what extends backwards, all those parts of the skeleton in the bird which appear similar to ribs and spine, all this is to

be looked upon as head—certainly metamorphosed and transformed—but nevertheless as head. The whole bird is really
head.

This is due to the fact that, to understand the bird, we
must go very, very far back in the planetary evolution of the
Earth. The bird has a long planetary history behind it, a
much longer planetary history than, for example, the camel.
The camel is an animal of much later origin than any bird.
Those birds which, like the ostrich, have been forced downwards to the Earth, were the latest to come into existence.
Those birds which live freely in the air—eagles, vultures—
are very ancient creatures of the Earth. In earlier Earth
epochs—Moon-epoch, Sun-epoch—they still possessed within
them what later developed from within outwards as far as
the skin, and later still formed itself into what you now see
in the feathers and the horny beak. What is outer in the bird
is of later origin, and came about through the fact that the
bird developed its head-nature comparatively early; and in
the conditions into which it came in later stages of Earth-
evolution, all that it could still add to this head-nature was
what lies in its plumage. This plumage was given to the birds
by the Moon and the Earth, whereas the rest of its nature
comes from much earlier epochs.

But all this has yet a much deeper side. Let us look at the
bird in the air—the eagle, let us say, in his majestic flight—
upon whom, as though by an outer gift of grace, the rays of
the sun and their action bestowed his plumage, bestowed his
horny beak—let us look at this eagle as he flies in the air.
Certain forces work upon him there. The sun does not only
possess the physical forces of light and warmth of which we
usually speak. When I described the Druid Mysteries to you,
I drew your attention to the fact that spiritual forces too
emanate from the sun. It is these forces which give to the
different species of birds their variegated colours, the special
formation of their plumage. When we penetrate with spiritual
perception into the nature of the sun's working, we understand why the eagle has his particular plumage and when we

deepen our contemplation of this being of the eagle, when we develop an inner, artistic comprehension of nature which contains the spiritual within it, when we can perceive how formative forces work out of the impulses of the sun— strengthened by other impulses of which I shall speak later— when we see how the sun-impulses stream down over the eagle even before he has emerged from the egg, how they conjure forth the plumage, or, to be more exact, how they conjure it into his fleshy form, then we can ask ourselves : What is the significance of all this for man? The significance of this for man is that it is what makes his brain into the bearer of thoughts. And you have the right insight into the Macrocosm, into Great Nature, when you so regard the eagle that you say : The eagle has his plumage, his bright, many-coloured feathers; in these lives the self-same force which lives in you in that you make your brain into the bearer of thoughts. What makes the convolutions of your brain? What makes your brain capable of taking up that inner salt-force which is the basis of thinking? What really enables your brain to make a thinker of you? It is the same force which gives his feathers to the eagle in the air. Thus we feel ourselves related to the eagle through the fact that we think : we feel the human substitute for the eagle's plumage within us. Our thoughts flow out from the brain in the same way as the feathers stream out from the eagle.*

When we ascend from the physical level to the astral level, we must make this paradoxical statement : on the physical plane the same forces bring about the formation of plumage as on the astral plane bring about the formation of thoughts. To the eagle they give the formation of feathers; that is the physical aspect of the formation of thoughts. To man they give thoughts; that is the astral aspect of the formation of feathers. Such things are sometimes indicated in a wonderful way in the genius of folk-language. If a feather is cut off at the top and what is inside extracted, country people call this

* Homer compares the speed of the Phaeacian ships to a *bird's wing or a thought. Odyssey* VII. 36.

the soul. Certainly many people will see in this name *soul* only an external description. It is not an external description. For those who have insight a feather contains something tremendous: it contains the secret of the formation of thoughts.

And now let us look away from what lives in the air, and, in order to have a representative example, let us consider a mammal such as the lion. We can really only understand the lion when we develop a feeling for the joy, the inner satisfaction the lion has in living together with his surroundings. There is indeed no animal, unless it be related to the lion, which has such wonderful, such mysterious breathing. In all creatures of the animal world the rhythms of breathing must harmonize with the rhythms of circulation; but whereas the rhythms of blood circulation become heavy through the digestive processes which are dependent on them, the rhythms of breathing become light because they strive to rise up to the lightness of the formation of the brain. In the case of the bird, what lives in its breathing actually lives simultaneously in its head. The bird is all head, and it presents its head outwardly, as it were, towards the world. Its thoughts are the forms of its plumage. For to one who has a feeling for the beauty of nature, there is hardly anything more moving than to feel the inner connection between man's thought—when it is really concrete, inwardly teeming with life—and the plumage of a bird. Anyone who is inwardly practised in such things knows quite exactly when he is thinking like a peacock, when he is thinking like an eagle, or when he is thinking like a sparrow. Apart from the fact that the one is astral and the other physical, these things do actually correspond in a wonderful way. And so it may be said that the bird's life in breathing preponderates to such a degree that the other processes—blood-circulation and so on—are almost negligible. All the heaviness of digestion, yes, even the heaviness of blood-circulation, is done away with in the bird's feeling of itself; it is not there.

In the lion a kind of balance exists between breathing and

blood-circulation. Certainly in the case of the lion the blood-circulation is weighed down, but not so much, let us say, as in the case of the camel or the ox. There the digestion burdens the blood-circulation to a remarkable degree. In the lion, whose digestive tract apparatus is comparatively short and is so formed that the digestive process is completed as rapidly as possible, digestion does not burden the circulation to any marked degree. On the other hand, it is also the case that in the lion's head the development of the head-nature is such that breathing is held in balance with the rhythm of circulation. The lion, more than any other animal, possesses an inner rhythm of breathing and rhythm of the heart-beat which are inwardly maintained in balance, which are inwardly harmonized. This is why the lion—when we think of what may be called his subjective life—has that particular way of devouring his food with unbridled voracity, why he literally gulps it down. For he is really only happy when he has swallowed it. He is ravenous for nourishment, because it lies in his nature that hunger causes him much more pain than it causes other animals. He is greedy for nourishment but he is not bent on being a fastidious gourmet! Enjoyment of the taste is not what possesses him, for he is an animal which finds its inner satisfaction in the equilibrium between breathing and blood-circulation. Only when the lion's food has passed over into the blood which regulates the heart-beat, and when the heart-beat has come into reciprocal action with the breathing—for it is a source of enjoyment to the lion when he draws in the breath-stream with deep inner satisfaction—only when he feels in himself the result of his feeding, this inner balance between breathing and blood-circulation, does the lion live in his own element. He lives fully as lion when he experiences the deep inner satisfaction of his blood beating upwards, of his breath pulsing downwards. And it is in this reciprocal crossing of two wave-pulsations that the lion really lives.

Picture the lion, how he runs, how he leaps, how he holds his head, even how he looks around him, and you will see that all this leads back to a continual rhythmic interplay between coming out of balance, and again coming into balance. There is perhaps hardly anything that can touch one in so mysterious a way as the remarkable gaze of the lion, from which so much looks out, something of inner mastery, the mastery of opposing forces. This is what looks out from the lion's gaze : the absolute and complete mastery of the heart-beat through the rhythm of the breath.

And again, let those who have a sense for the artistic understanding of forms look at the form of the lion's mouth, revealing as it does how the heart-beat pulses upwards towards the mouth, but is held back by the breath. If you could really picture this reciprocal contact of heart-beat and breathing, you would arrive at the form of the lion's mouth.

The lion is all breast-organ. He is the animal in which the rhythmic system is brought to perfect expression both in outer form and in way of living. The lion is so organized that this inter-action of heart-beat and breathing is also brought to expression in the reciprocal relationship of heart and lungs.

So we must say : When we look in the human being for what most closely resembles the bird, though naturally metamorphosed, it is the human head; when we look in the human being for what most closely resembles the lion, it is the region of the human breast, where the rhythms meet each other, the rhythms of circulation and breathing.

And now let us turn our attention away from all that belongs in the upper air to the bird-kingdom; away from all that lives in the circulation of the air immediately adjacent to the Earth, as does the lion; let us consider the ox or cow. In other connections I have often spoken of how enchanting it is to contemplate a herd of cattle, replete and satisfied, lying down in a meadow; to observe this process of digestion which here again is expressed in the position of the body, in the expression of the eyes, in every movement. Take an opportunity of observing a cow lying in the meadow, if from here or there some kind of noise disturbs her. It is really wonderful to see how the cow raises her head, how in this lifting there lies the feeling that it is all heaviness, that it is not easy for the cow to lift the head, as though something very special were within it. When we see a cow in the meadow disturbed in this way, we cannot but say to ourselves : This cow is astonished that she must lift her head for anything but grazing. Why do I lift my head now? I am not grazing, and there is no point in lifting my head unless it is to graze. Only look at the way she does it! All this is to be seen in the way the cow lifts her head. But it is not only in the movement of the lifting of the head. (You cannot imagine the lion lifting his head as the cow does.) It lies also in the form of the head. And if we further observe the animal's whole form, we see it is in fact what I may call an extended digestive system! The weight of the digestion burdens the blood-circulation to such a degree that it overwhelms everything to do with head and breathing. The animal is all digestion. It is infinitely wonderful, when looked at spiritually, to turn one's gaze upwards to the bird, and then to look downwards upon the cow.

Of course, to whatever height one might raise the cow, physically she would never be a bird. But if one could pass over what is physical in the cow—first bringing her into the moisture of the air in the immediate vicinity of the earth, and transforming her etheric form into one corresponding to the moisture; and, next, raising her up higher, bringing her as far as the astral, then up in the heights the cow would be a bird. Astrally she would be a bird.

And you see, it is just here that something wonderful approaches us, if we have insight, compelling us to say: What the bird up in the heights has astrally out of its astral body, what works there, as I have said, upon the formation of its plumage, this the cow has embodied in her flesh, in her muscles, in her bones. What is astral in the bird has become physical in the cow. The appearance is of course different in the astrality, but so it is.

On the other hand, if I reverse the process, and allow what belongs to the astrality of a bird to sink down, thereby bringing about the transformation into the etheric and physical, the eagle would become a cow, because what is astral in the eagle is incorporated into the flesh, into the bodily nature of the cow as she lies on the ground engaged in digestion; for it belongs to this digestive process in the cow to develop a wonderful astrality. The cow becomes beautiful in the process of digestion. Seen astrally, something immensely beautiful lies in this digestion. And when it is said by ordinary philistine concepts, indeed by philistine idealism, that the process of digestion is the most lowly, this must be indicted as untruth, when, from a higher vantage-point, one gazes with spiritual sight at this digestive process in the cow. For this is beautiful, this is grand, this is something of an immense spirituality.

The lion does not attain to this spirituality, much less the bird. In the bird the digestive process is something almost entirely physical. One does of course find the etheric body in the digestive system of the bird, but in its digestive processes one finds very little, indeed almost nothing, of astrality. On the other hand, something is present in the digestive processes of the cow which, seen astrally, is quite stupendous, an entire world.

And now, if we wish to look at what is similar in man, again seeking for the correspondence between what is developed in the cow in a one-sided way, the physical embodiment of a certain astrality, we find this in man—harmoniously adjusted to the other parts of his organism, woven, as it were, into his digestive organs and their continuation—in the limb-system. So in truth what I behold high in the upper air in the eagle; what I behold in the realm where the animal rejoices in the air around him as in the case of the lion; and what I behold when the animal is bound up with the subterrestrial earth-forces, which project their working into its digestive organs (as occurs when I look away from the heights into the depths, and bring my understanding to bear on the nature and being of the cow) all these three forms I find united into a harmony in man, into reciprocal balance. I find the metamorphosis of the bird in the human head, the metamorphosis of the lion in the human breast, the metamorphosis of the cow in the digestive system and the system of the limbs— though naturally metamorphosed, tremendously transformed.

When today we contemplate these things and realize that man is actually born out of the whole of nature, that he bears the whole of nature within himself as I have shown, that he bears the bird-kingdom, the lion-kingdom, the essential being of the cow within him, then we get the separate component parts of what is expressed in the abstract sentence : Man is a "Little World". He is indeed a Little World, and the Great World is within him; and all the creatures which live above in the air, and the animals on the face of the earth whose special element is the air which circulates around them, and the animals which have their special element below the surface of the earth, as it were, in the forces of weight—all these work together in man as a harmonious whole. So that man is in truth the synthesis of eagle, lion, and ox or cow.

When one discovers this again through the investigations of a more modern Spiritual Science, one gains that great respect of which I have often spoken for the old, instinctive, clairvoyant insight into the Cosmos. Then, for instance, one gains a great respect for the mighty imagination that man consists of eagle, lion, and cow or ox, which, harmonized in true proportion, together form the human being in his totality.

But before I pass on—this may be tomorrow—to discuss the separate impulses which lie in the forces weaving around the eagle, around the lion, around the cow, I want to speak of another correspondence between man's inner being and what is outside in the Cosmos.

From what we already know we can now take a further step. The human head seeks for what accords with its nature : it must direct its gaze upwards to the bird-kingdom. If one is to understand the human breast—the heart-beat, the breathing—as a secret within the secrets of nature, the gaze must be turned to something of the nature of the lion. And man

must try to understand his digestive system from the constitution, from the organization, of the ox or cow. But in his
head man has the bearer of his thoughts, in the breast the
bearer of his feelings, in his digestive system the bearer of his
will. So that in his soul-nature, too, man is an image of the
thoughts which weave through the world with the birds and
find expression in their plumage, and of the world of feeling
encircling the earth, which is to be found in the lion in the
balanced life of heart-beat and breathing and which, though
milder in man, does indeed represent the inner quality of
courage—the Greek language made use of the word εὐψυχία *
for the qualities of heart and breast, the inner quality of
courage in man. And if man wishes to find his will-impulses
which, when he gives them external form, are predominantly
connected with the metabolism, he must turn his gaze to the
bodily form in the cow.

What today sounds grotesque or paradoxical, what may
seem almost insane to an age that has retained absolutely no
understanding for the relationships of the world, does nevertheless contain a truth which points back to ancient customs.
It is a striking phenomenon that Mahatma Gandhi—who has
now been presented to the world, more falsely than truly, by
Romain Rolland in a rather unpleasant book—that Mahatma
Gandhi, who certainly turns his activity in an outward direction, but at the same time stands within the Indian people,
somewhat like a rationalist of the eighteenth century over
against the ancient Hindu religion—it is striking that in his
rationalized Hinduism Gandhi retains the veneration of the
cow. This cannot be set aside, says Mahatma Gandhi, who,
as you know, was sentenced by the English to six years' im-
prisonment for his political activity in India. He still retains
veneration for the cow.

Things such as these, which have so tenaciously retained
their position in spiritual cultures, can only be understood
when one is aware of the inner connections, when one really
knows what tremendous secrets lie in the ruminating animal,

* The quality of the "great soul", cf. *Coeur de Lion*.

the cow; and how one can venerate in it a lofty astrality, which has, as it were, become earthly, and only thereby more lowly. Such things enable us to understand the religious veneration which is paid to the cow in Hinduism, and which the whole bevy of rationalistic and intellectualistic concepts which have been brought to bear on this subject will never enable us to understand.

And so we see how will, feeling, thought, can be looked for outside in the Cosmos, and correspondingly in the microcosm, man.

There are, however, all kinds of other forces in the human being, and all kinds of other forces outside in nature too. So now I must ask you to consider for the moment the metamorphoses undergone by the creature which later becomes a butterfly.

You know the butterfly lays its egg. Out of the egg comes the caterpillar. The egg contains everything that is the germinal essence of the later butterfly. The caterpillar emerges from the egg into the light-irradiated air. This is the environment into which the caterpillar comes. You must, therefore, envisage how the caterpillar really lives in this sunlit air.

Here you must consider what happens when you are lying in bed at night and have lit the lamp, and a moth flies towards the lamp, and finds its death in the light. This light works upon the moth in such a way that it subjects itself to a search for death. Here we have an example of the action of light upon the living. The innocent image of the moth

Now the caterpillar—I am only indicating these things shortly today; tomorrow and the next day we shall consider them somewhat more exactly—the caterpillar cannot rise up to the source of light, to the Sun, in order to cast itself into it, but it would like to do so. Its desire to do so is just as strong as the moth's, which casts itself into the flame of your bedside lamp, and there meets its death. The moth casts itself into the flame and finds its death in physical fire. The caterpillar seeks the flame just as eagerly, the flame which comes towards it from the Sun. But it cannot throw itself into the

Sun; the passing over into warmth, into light, remains for the caterpillar something spiritual. It is as spiritual activity that the whole action of the Sun works upon the caterpillar. It follows each ray of the Sun, this caterpillar; by day it accompanies the rays of the Sun. Just as the moth throws itself at once into the flame, giving over its whole moth-substance to the light, so the caterpillar weaves its caterpillar-substance slowly into the light, pauses at night, weaves by day, and spins and weaves around itself the whole cocoon. And we have in the cocoon, in the threads of the cocoon, what the caterpillar weaves out of its own substance as it spins on in the flooding sunlight. And now the caterpillar, which has become a chrysalis, has woven around itself, out of its own substance, the rays of the Sun, which it has incorporated in itself. The moth is consumed quickly in the physical fire. The caterpillar, sacrificing itself, casts itself into the sunlight, and from moment to moment weaves around itself the threads of the Sun's rays which it follows in their course. If you look at the cocoon of the silkworm you are looking at woven sunlight, only the sunlight is embodied through the substance of the silk-spinning caterpillar itself. Now the space it inhabits is inwardly enclosed. The outer sunlight has in a sense been overcome. That part of the sunlight to which I referred when I described the Druidic Mysteries,* as entering into the cromlechs, is now inside the cocoon. The Sun, which previously exerted its physical power, causing the caterpillar to spin its own cocoon, now exerts its power upon what is inside, and from out of this it creates the butterfly, which now emerges. Then the whole circle begins anew. Here you have separated out before you in sequence what is, as it were, compressed in the egg of a bird.

Compare this whole process with what happens when a bird lays its eggs. Inside the bird itself, still through a process of metamorphosis, the chalky egg-shell is formed around the egg. The forces of the sunlight make use of the substance of

* In a lecture to workmen on 11th September, 1923. See also *The Evolution of Consciousness*, Lectures 8 and 9 (Rudolf Steiner Press).

the chalk to press together the whole sequence of what here in the butterfly is separated off into egg, caterpillar, cocoon. All these processes are compressed at the place where, in the bird's egg, the hard shell forms itself around them. Through this pressing together of processes which otherwise are separated into different stages, the whole embryonic development in the bird is different. All that up to this point of the third stage is completed within the bird, in the butterfly is separated into egg-formation, caterpillar-formation, chrysalis-formation, cocoon-formation. Here all can be seen outwardly, until the butterfly slips out.

And when one now follows the whole process astrally, what is to be seen then? Well, the bird in its whole formation represents the human head, the organ of thought-formation. What does the butterfly represent, the butterfly which in its embryonic formation is so extraordinarily complicated? We find that the butterfly represents a continuation of the function of the head, it represents the forces of the head spread out, as it were, over the whole human body. Here something happens in the whole human being, corresponding to a process in nature but different from the process of the formation of the bird.

When we take into account its etheric and astral nature, we have in the human head something very similar to egg-formation, only metamorphosed. If we had only the function of the head we should form nothing but momentary thoughts. Our thoughts would not sink down more deeply into us, involve the whole human being, and then rise up again as memories. If I look at the momentary thoughts which I form of the outer world, and then look up to the eagle, I say: In the eagle's plumage I see outside myself embodied thoughts; within me these remain as thoughts, but only momentary thoughts. But if I look at what I bear within me as my memories, I find a more complicated process. Deep in the physical body, though certainly in a spiritual way, a kind of egg-formation is taking place. In the etheric this certainly represents something quite different, something which in its external physical aspect resembles the caterpillar-formation. In the astral body, however, in its inner aspect, it is similar to the chrysalis-formation, the cocoon-formation. And when I have a percept which evokes a thought in me, what loosens, ejects, as it were, that thought and presses it downward is like the butterfly laying an egg. The development is then similar to what takes place in the caterpillar; the life in the etheric body offers itself up to the spiritual light, weaves around the thoughts, as it were, an inner astral cocoon-web, from which the memories slip out. If we see the bird's plumage manifested in momentary thoughts, so we must see the butterfly's wings, shimmering with colour, manifested in our memory-thoughts in a spiritual way.

Thus we look around and feel to what an immense degree nature is related to us. We think and see the world of thoughts in the flying birds. We remember, we have memories, and see the world of memory-pictures, living within us, in the fluttering butterflies shimmering in the sunlight. Yes, man is a Microcosm, and contains within himself the secrets of the Great World outside. And it is a fact that what we perceive inwardly—our thoughts, our feelings, our will-impulses, our memory-pictures, when regarded from the other side, from without, in a macrocosmic sense, can all be recognized again in the kingdom of nature.

This is to look at reality. Reality of this kind does not allow itself to be grasped by mere thoughts, for to mere thoughts reality is a matter of indifference; they only hold to logic. But this same logic can prove the most contradictory things in the sphere of reality. To make this apparent, let me close with an illustration which will serve to form a bridge to what we shall consider tomorrow.

A certain tribe of African negroes, the Felatas, have a very beautiful fable, from which much can be learned.

Once upon a time a lion, a wolf and a hyena set out upon a journey. They met an antelope. The antelope was torn to pieces by one of the animals. The three travellers were good friends, so now the question arose as to how to divide the dismembered antelope between them. First the lion spoke to the hyena, saying, "You divide it." The hyena possessed his logic. He is the animal who deals not with the living but with the dead. His logic is naturally determined by the measure of his courage, or rather of his cowardice. According to whether this courage is more or less, he approaches reality in different ways. The hyena said: "We will divide the antelope into three equal parts—one for the lion, one for the wolf, and one for myself." Whereupon the lion fell upon the hyena and killed him. Now the hyena was out of the way, and again it was a question of sharing out the antelope. So the lion said to the wolf, "See, my dear wolf, now we must share it out differently. You divide it. How would you share it out?" Then the wolf said, "Yes, we must now apportion it differently; it cannot be shared out evenly as before. As you have rid us of the hyena, you as lion must get the first third; the second third would have been yours in any case, as the hyena said, and the remaining third you must get because you are the wisest and bravest of all the animals." This is how the wolf apportioned it. Then said the lion, "Who taught you to divide in this way?" To which the wolf replied, "The hyena taught me." So the lion did not devour the wolf, but, according to the wolf's logic, took the three portions for himself.

Yes, the mathematics, the intellectual element, was the same in the hyena and the wolf. They divided the antelope into three parts. But they applied this intellect, this calculation, to reality in a different way. Thereby destiny, too, was essentially altered. The hyena was devoured because his application of the principle of division to reality had different results from that of the wolf who was not devoured. For the wolf related his hyena-logic—he even said himself that the hyena had taught it to him—to quite another reality. He related it to reality in such a way that the lion no longer felt compelled to devour him too.

You see, hyena-logic in the first case, hyena-logic also in the wolf; but in its application to reality the intellectual logical element resulted in something quite different.

It is thus with all abstractions. You can do everything in the world with abstractions just according to whether you relate them to reality in this or that way. We must, therefore, be able to penetrate with insight into a reality such as the correspondence between man, as Microcosm, and the Macrocosm. We must be able to study the human being not with logic only, but in a sense which can never be achieved unless intellectualism is led over into the artistic element of the world. But if you succeed in bringing about the metamorphosis of intellectualism into artistic comprehension, and are able to develop the artistic into the principle of knowledge, then you find what is within man in a human way, not in a natural way, outside in the Macrocosm, in the Great World. Then you find the relationship of the human being to the Great World in a true and real sense.

LECTURE II

20th October, 1923

Having considered in the lecture yesterday the nature of the animals of the heights, represented by the eagle, the animals of the middle region, represented by the lion, and the animals of the earth-depths, represented by the ox or cow, we can today turn our attention to man's connection with the universe from that particular aspect which reveals the inner structural relationship of the human being to these representatives of the animal world.

Let us first turn our gaze to the upper regions, about which we said yesterday that when the animal derives its particular forces from them, they do then in fact cause the whole animal to become head-organization. There we see how the bird owes its very being to the sun-irradiated atmosphere. This sun-irradiated atmosphere—everything, that is to say, which can be absorbed by the bird through the fact that it owes the most important part of its being to it—is a necessity to the bird. And I told you yesterday that it is upon this that the actual formation of the plumage depends. The bird has its actual being within. What is brought about in the bird by the outer world is embodied in its plumage. But when the influence of this sun-irradiated air is not impressed on the being from without, as in the case of the eagle, but is activated within, as in the case of the human nervous system, then thoughts arise—momentary thoughts, as I said, thoughts of the immediate present.

When we thus turn our gaze upwards to the heights, and are filled with all that results from such a contemplation, it is to the tranquil atmosphere and to the streaming sunlight that our attention is drawn. We must not, however, think of the sun in isolation. The sun maintains its power through the fact that it comes into connection with the different regions of the universe. Human knowledge has expressed this relationship by connecting the sun activities with the so-called animal circle or zodiac, so that when the sunlight falls to earth from Leo, from Libra or from Scorpio, its significance also signifies something different for the earth according to whether it is strengthened or weakened by the other planets of our planetary system. And here different relationships arise in regard to the different planets; the relationships in regard to the so-called outer planets, Mars, Jupiter, Saturn, are different from those in regard to the so-called inner planets, Mercury, Venus and Moon.

If we now consider the organization of the eagle, it is most important first of all to observe how far the Sun-forces become modified, strengthened or weakened, by their interaction with Saturn, Jupiter, Mars. It is not for nothing that legend speaks of the eagle as the bird of Jupiter. In general Jupiter stands as the representative of the outer planets. And if we were to draw a diagram illustrating what is meant here, we would have to draw the sphere which Saturn has in world-space, in the cosmos, as also that of Jupiter and Mars.

Let us draw this, so that we may actually see it, in a diagram* : the Saturn sphere, the Jupiter sphere, the Mars sphere; then we find the transition to the Sun sphere, giving us in the outermost part of our planetary system the working together of Sun, Mars, Jupiter, Saturn.

And when we see the eagle circling in the air we do in fact utter a reality when we say: These forces which stream through the air from the Sun in such a way that they are composed of the working together of Sun with Mars, Jupiter and Saturn—these forces are those which live in the whole structure, in the very being of the eagle. But at the same time they live in the formation of the human head. And when we place man into the universe in accordance with his true nature—on earth he is only, so to speak, a miniature picture

* See next page.

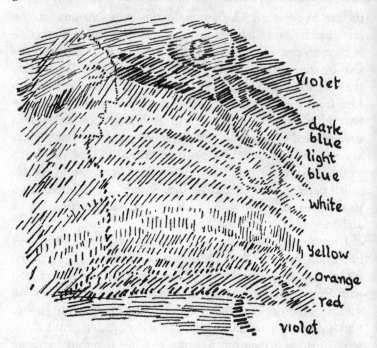

Violet
dark blue
light blue
white
Yellow
Orange
red
violet

of himself—as regards his head we must place him into the eagle-sphere.

We must, therefore, think of Man in regard to his head as belonging to the eagle-sphere; and therewith we have indicated that element in the human being which is connected with the upward tending forces.

The lion is the representative of those animals which are in the real sense Sun-animals, in which the sun unfolds its own special force. The lion prospers best when the constellations above the sun and the constellations below the sun are so ordered that they exert the least influence upon the sun itself. Then those special characteristics appear which I described to you yesterday, namely that the forces of the sun itself, permeating the air, produce in the lion a breathing system of just such a kind that in its rhythm it is in perfect balance with the rhythm of the blood-circulation, not as regards number but as regards its dynamic. In the lion this balances itself out in a wonderfully beautiful way. The lion regulates his blood-circulation through the breathing, and the blood-circulation continually stimulates the stream of the breath. I told you that this can be seen even in the form, in the very structure of the lion's mouth. In this form itself the wonderful relationship between the rhythm of the blood and the rhythm of the breath is actually expressed. One can see this, too, in the remarkable gaze of the lion, resting in itself, and yet turned boldly outwards.

But what lives in the lion's gaze lives also in the other elements of human nature, the metabolic system, the head system, and the breast or heart system, that is the rhythmic system of Man.

And if we picture the special Sun-activity we must so draw the diagram of the human being that we place his heart, and the lungs connected to it, into the region of this Sun-activity. It is here, in this sphere, that we have the lion-nature in man.

When we turn to the inner planets nearer the earth, we have first the Mercury sphere. This has to do in particular with the finer parts of the digestive organism of man, the region where the foodstuffs are transformed into lymphatic substance, which is then carried into the circulation of the blood.

Progressing further, we come into the region of Venus-activity. This is connected with the somewhat coarser parts of man's digestive system, to that part of the human organism which works primarily from the stomach upon the foodstuffs which have been taken in. We next come into the sphere of the Moon. (I am drawing this in the sequence customary today in astronomy; I could also draw it differently.) There we enter that region where those digestive processes which are connected with the Moon act and re-act upon the human being.

In this way we have placed man into the entire universe. By turning our minds to those cosmic activities which the Sun carries out in conjunction with Mercury, Venus, Moon, we come into the region containing the forces which are taken up by the order of the animals represented for us by the cow, in the sense which I spoke of yesterday. There we have what the Sun cannot do by itself alone, but what the Sun can only do when its own forces are conducted to the earth by means of the planets which are nearest to the earth. When these forces are all at work, when they do not only stream through the air, but penetrate through the earth's surface in various ways, then these forces work up again from the earth depths. And what thus works up from earth depths belongs to the sphere which we see embodied outwardly in the organism of the cow.

The cow is the animal of digestion. It is, moreover, the animal which accomplishes digestion in such a way that there lies in its digestive processes the earthly reflection of something actually super-earthly; its whole digestive process is permeated with an astrality which reflects the entire cosmos in a wonderful light-filled way. There is—as I said yesterday—a whole world in this astral organism of the cow, but everything is heavy, everything is so organized that the weight of the earth works there. You have only to consider that the cow is obliged to consume an eighth of her weight in food-stuffs each day. Man can be satisfied with a fortieth part and remain healthy. Thus the cow needs earth-gravity in order fully to meet the needs of her organism. Her organism is orientated towards this need for the weight of matter. Every day the cow must digest an eighth of her weight. This binds the cow with her material substance to the earth, whereas, through her astrality she is at the same time an image of the heights, of the cosmos.

This is why, as I said yesterday, the cow is an object of so much veneration for those who confess to the Hindu religion. The Hindu says to himself : The cow lives here on the earth; but through this fact she forms in solid physical substance an image of something super-earthly. It is indeed the case that man's nature is organized in a normal way when he can bring into harmony these three cosmic activities manifested

in a one-sided way in eagle, lion and cow; when he himself
is the confluence of the activities of eagle, lion and cow.

In accordance with the general course of world events,
however, we are now living in an age when the evolution
of the world is threatened by a certain danger; and this
danger will—if I may so express myself—actually take effect
in man also in a one-sided way. From the fourteenth and
fifteenth centuries up to our own day the facts of human
earthly evolution are such that, to an ever increasing degree,
the eagle activities wish to make one-sided claims upon the
human head, the lion activities upon the human rhythmic
system, and the cow activities upon the human metabolism
and upon all man's activity on the earth.

This is the stamp of our age, that it is the aim of the cosmic
powers to bring about a threefold division of man, and that
each form of these cosmic powers is always striving to sup-
press the others. The eagle strives to subjugate the lion and
the cow and make them of no account, and in like manner
with each of the other elements. Just in our present age
something particularly alluring is working upon the subconscious in man; alluring because in a certain sense there is
also something beautiful about it. In his conscious life man
today is unaware of this but, for his subconsciousness, three
calls surge and sound through the world seeking to tempt him
with their allurement. And I must say that it is the secret of
our present time that, from the sphere of the eagle, there
sounds down to man what actually gives the eagle his eagle
nature, what gives him his plumage, what hovers around him
as astrality. It is the eagle nature itself which becomes audible
for the subconsciousness of man. This is the alluring call :

> Learn to know my nature !
> I give thee the power
> To create a universe
> In thine own head.

Thus speaks the eagle. That is the call from above, which
today wishes to impose one-sidedness upon man.

And there is a second alluring call. This is the call which comes to us from the middle region, where the forces of the cosmos form the lion-nature, where, through the mingling of sun and air, they bring about that equilibrium between the rhythms of breathing and blood-circulation which constitutes the nature of the lion. What thus vibrates through the air, from the nature of the lion, what wills to make man's own rhythmic system one-sided, this today speaks alluringly to man's subconsciousness, saying :

> Learn to know my nature!
> I give thee the power
> To embody the universe
> In the radiance* of the encircling air.

Thus speaks the lion.

These voices, which speak to man's subconsciousness, have more effect than is supposed. Yes, my dear friends, there are certain human natures on earth organized in such a way that they are particularly liable to absorb their influences. Thus, for instance, all those who populate the west are so organized that they are specially prone to be allured, to be led astray, by the voice of the eagle. Thus American civilization, on account of the special organization of its people, is particularly exposed to the temptation offered by what the eagle speaks. And Central Europe, which is imbued with much of the culture of classical antiquity, which contains so much of what caused Goethe, for instance, to make his journey to Italy, a journey which acted on his life like a liberation— central Europe is particularly exposed to what is uttered by the lion.

Oriental civilization is pre-eminently exposed to what is uttered by the cow. And just as both other animals give utterance in their cosmic representation, so there sounds upwards from earth-depths, like a rumbling, muffled roaring, the call of what lies in the heaviness of the cow. It is actually the case, as I described to you yesterday, that when one sees a

* German *Schein* for which there is no exact English equivalent.

herd of cattle replete with grazing, sees them as they lie there in their own peculiar way, their very form revealing that they are given over to earth-gravity, then all this is conditioned by the fact that this bodily form must assimilate daily an eighth of its own weight. And to this must be added that the earth-depths, which, under the influence of Sun, Mercury, Venus and Moon, bring all this about in the digestive system of the cow—that these earth-depths, as if with demonic rumbling power, resound through such a herd with the words:

> Learn to know my nature!
> I give thee the power
> To wrest from the universe
> Measure, number and weight.

Thus speaks the cow. And it is the orient which is specially exposed to the allurement of this call. What is meant here, however, is that, though it is the orient which is primarily exposed to this alluring call of the cow on account of the ancient veneration of the cow in Hinduism, yet, if this allurement were actually so to seize hold of mankind that what arises from this call would gain the mastery, then these influences emanating from the orient would produce a civilization, which, spreading over centre and west, would hinder progress and engender decadence. The demonic earth-forces would work in a one-sided way upon earth-civilization. What then would actually happen?

The following would happen. In the course of the last centuries, under the influence of a technology brought about by external science, an external technological life has come about on the earth. Certainly our technical achievement is wonderful in every sphere. But in technology nature forces work in their lifeless form. And the important factors in bringing these lifeless nature forces into play so absolutely and utterly that they would impose a stratum of civilization over the earth—these factors are number, measure and weight.

The scales, the measuring rod—to weigh, to count, to measure—these are the ideal of the modern scientist, of the modern technician, whose entire profession is actually dependent upon external science. We have brought things to such a pass that an important mathematician of our times, in response to the question : What is the guarantee of existence?, gives the following answer. (Philosophers of all ages have tried to answer the question : What is actually real?) This important physicist says : What can be measured is real; what cannot be measured is unreal. The ideal is to regard all being in such a way that it can be brought into the laboratory, and weighed, measured and counted; and from what is weighed, measured and counted, science, or what stands for it, is constructed. All this then streams out into technology. Number, measure and weight have become the standards of the whole of civilization.

Now as long as people only apply themselves with their ordinary understanding to measure, number and weight, things are not particularly bad. People are certainly very clever, but they are still a long way from being as clever as the universe. And this is why things cannot become particularly bad so long as, in comparison with the universe, they go about the measuring, weighing and counting in a dilettante way. But if present-day civilization were to be transformed into *initiation,* things would be bad indeed, if this attitude of mind remained. And this can happen if the civilization of the west, which stands entirely under the sign of measure, number and weight, were to be flooded by what might well come to pass in the east, namely, that through initiation-science people might fathom what actually lives spiritually in the organism of the cow. For if you penetrate into the organism of the cow, burdened with earthly heaviness, with this eighth of her weight in foodstuffs, with all that can be weighed, measured and counted, you learn what is being organized spiritually in the cow by this earth-heaviness, you learn to understand the whole organism of the cow as it lies in the meadow digesting, and in this process of digestion manifesting wonderful revelations from the astrality of the universe. Then you learn how to form what can be

weighed, measured and counted into a system with which
you could overcome all other forms of civilization and impose
upon the whole earth-globe one civilization, which would do
nothing but weigh, count and measure, making everything
else disappear. For what would result from initiation into the
organization of the cow? That is a question of utmost gravity,
a question of immense significance. What would be the result?

Well, the whole way in which people construct machines
varies greatly according to the nature of the machine in question; but everything tends towards the gradual development
of these still imperfect, primitive machines into a kind of
machine which depends upon vibrations, and where the aim
is to make the machines effective by means of vibrations or
oscillations, by means of movements which run a periodic
course. Everything is hastening towards such machines. But
if once these machines in their co-ordinated activity could be
constructed in such a way as can be learned from the distribution of foodstuffs in the organization of the cow, then
the vibrations which would be conjured up on the earth-
globe through the machines, these small earth-vibrations,
would so run their course that what is above the earth would
sound together with, vibrate together with what is happening
on the earth; so that our planetary system in its movements
would be compelled to vibrate with our earth-system, just as
a string tuned to a certain pitch vibrates in sympathy when
another one is struck in the same room.

That is the terrible law of the sounding in unison of vibrations which would be fulfilled if the alluring call of the cow
would so decoy the orient that it would then be able to penetrate in an absolutely convincing way into the unspiritual,
purely mechanistic civilization of the west and centre; and
thereby it would become possible to conjure up on the earth
a mechanistic system fitting exactly into the mechanistic
system of the universe. Through this everything connected
with the working of air, with the forces of the circumference,
and everything connected with the working of the stars,
would be exterminated from human civilization. What man

experiences, for instance, through the cycle of the year, what he experiences through living together with the sprouting, budding life of spring, with the fading, dying life of autumn —all this would lose its import for him. Human civilization would resound with the clattering and rattling of the vibrating machines and with the echo of this clattering and rattling which would stream down upon the earth from the cosmos as a reaction to this mechanisation of the earth. *Japan*

If you observe a part of what is active at the present time, you will say to yourselves : A part of our present-day civilization is actually on the way to having this terrible element of degeneracy as its goal.

Now turn your thoughts to what would happen if the centre fell a prey to the allurements of what is spoken by the lion. Then, it is true, the danger I have just described would not be present. Then mechanism would gradually disappear from the face of the earth. Civilization would not become mechanistic, but, with a one-sided power, man would be given over to all that lives in wind and weather, in the cycle of the year. Man would be yoked to the year's course, and thereby compelled to live particularly in the interaction of his rhythms of breathing and blood-circulation. He would develop in himself what his involuntary life can give him. He would primarily develop his breast-nature. Through this, however, such human egoism would come over earth civilization that everyone would be intent upon living for himself alone, that no-one would bother about anything save his own immediate well-being. It is this temptation to which the civilization of the centre is exposed, such is the existence which could hang like a fate over the civilization of the earth. *Europe*.

And yet again, if the alluring call of the eagle were to seduce the west, so that it would succeed in spreading its way of thinking and attitude of mind over the whole earth, binding itself up in a one-sided way in this kind of thinking and mental attitude, then, in mankind as a whole there would arise the urge to enter into connection with the super-earthly world, as this once was, as it was in the beginning, at the

outset of earth-evolution. People would feel the urge to extin-
guish what man has won for himself in freedom and independence. They would come to live only and entirely in that
unconscious will which allows the gods to live in human
muscles and nerves. They would revert to primitive conditions, to original, primitive clairvoyance. Man would seek to
free himself from the earth by turning back to earth-
beginnings. *California*

And I must say that, for exact clairvoyant vision, this is
further emphasized through the fact that man is continually
approached by what may be called the voice of the grazing
cow, which says: "Do not look upwards; all power comes *Ahriman*
from the earth. Learn to know all that lies in earth-activity.
Thou shalt become the lord of the earth. Thou shalt perpetu-
ate the results of thy work on earth." Yes, if man were to
succumb to this alluring call, it would be impossible to avoid
the danger of which I have spoken : the mechanizing of earth-
civilization. For the astrality of this animal of digestion wills
to make the present enduring, to make the present eternal.
From the lion-organization proceeds not what wills to make
the present endure, but rather what would make the present
as fleeting as possible, what would make everything a mere
sport of the cycle of the year, always repeating itself, what
would spend itself in wind and weather, in the play of the
sunbeams, in the currents of the air. And civilization, too,
would take on this character. *Rock music !*

If, with real understanding, one contemplates the eagle as
he soars through the air, it appears as though he were bear-
ing upon his plumage the memory of what was there at the
very inception of the earth. He has preserved in his plumage
the forces which have still worked into the earth from above.
It can be said that in every eagle we see the past mil-
lenia of the earth; with his physical nature he has not touched
the earth, or at the most only for the purpose of seizing his
prey, and in no way for the satisfaction of his own life. To
fulfil his own life the eagle circles in the air, because he is
indifferent to what has developed on the earth, because he

has his joy and inspiration from the forces of the air, because he actually despises the life of earth and wishes to live in that same element in which the earth itself lived when it was not yet earth, but when, in the beginning of its evolution, it was still imbuing itself with heavenly forces. The eagle is the proud creature which would not partake in the evolution of the solid earth, which withdrew from the influence of this solidifying process, and wished to remain united only with those forces which were there at the inception of the earth. *Lucifer*

Such are the teachings given to us by this threefold representation of the animal kingdom, if we can conceive it as an immense and mighty script, written into the universe for the elucidation of its riddles. For, in very truth, every single thing in the universe is a written character if we could but read it. And especially when we can read their connection do we understand the riddle of the universe.

How full of significance it is to have to realize : What we do when we measure with the compasses or measuring rod, when we weigh with the scales, when we count—this is in fact only a putting together of something which is fragmentary; it becomes a whole when we understand the organization of the cow in its inner spirituality. This means to read in the secrets of the universe. And this reading in the secrets of the universe leads into the understanding of the being of the world and of man. This is modern initiation wisdom. It is this which must be uttered at the present time from out of the depths of spiritual life.

It is difficult indeed today for man to be really man. For, if I may put it so, in face of the three animal types, man conducts himself like the antelope in the fable which I told you yesterday. What wills to be one-sided takes on a particular form. The lion remains lion, but he wishes to have his fellow beasts of prey as metamorphoses of the other animal representatives. Thus for what in truth is eagle he substitutes a fellow beast of prey, the hyena, whose nature it is to live upon what is dead, upon that element of death which is induced in our head, and which continually, at every moment, contributes atomistic particles towards our death. So this fable replaces the eagle with the hyena, the hyena which consumes decay; and in the place of the cow—in line with the degeneration—the lion puts his fellow beast of prey, the wolf. Thus we have in the fable the other threefold animal group, the lion, the hyena, the wolf. And as today the alluring calls stand over against each other, their cosmic symbolism is confronted with its opposite, in that, when the alluring calls resound, the eagle sinks to earth and becomes the hyena, and the cow no longer desires in her holy, humble way to be an image of the cosmos, but becomes the ravening wolf.

And now we can translate the legend with which I ended my lecture yesterday from the negro version into that of modern civilization. Yesterday I had to narrate this legend from what may be called the negro point of view: The lion, the wolf and the hyena went out hunting. They killed an antelope. First the hyena was asked to divide the prey; he apportioned it according to hyena-logic, and said: "A third for everyone: a third for the lion, a third for the wolf, and a third for me." Whereupon the hyena was consumed. And now the lion said to the wolf, "You divide it." So the wolf said, "You get the first third because you have killed the hyena, and therefore the hyena's share is also your due. The second third is yours because, according to the verdict of the hyena, you would have had a third in any case, for each of us was to have had a third; and you get the last third as well, because of all the beasts you are the wisest and bravest." And the lion said to the wolf, "Who taught you to divide in so excellent a way?" The wolf said, "The hyena taught it me."

The logic is the same in both cases, but in its application to reality something quite different results according to whether the hyena, or the wolf with the hyena's experience, applied the logic. It is in the application of logic to reality that the essential matter lies.

Now we can also translate this fable into what I may call the version of modern civilization and tell the story somewhat differently. But please notice that what I am telling is in terms of the whole development of the great course of culture. Thus, expressed in modern fashion, the story could perhaps run as follows: The antelope is killed. The hyena withdraws and delivers a silent verdict; he does not dare to arouse the growling of the lion. He draws back, delivers a silent verdict, and waits in the background. The lion and the wolf now begin to fight for the body of the antelope. They fight and fight, until they have so severely wounded each other that both die from their wounds. Now comes the hyena, and consumes antelope, wolf and lion, after they have entered into a state of decay. The hyena is the image of what lies in the human intellect, the element in human nature which kills. He is the reverse side, the caricature, of the eagle civilization.

If you feel what I wish to convey by the europeanizing of the old negro fable, you will understand that just at the present time these things should be rightly understood. But they will only be rightly understood when, in opposition to the threefold alluring call—the call of the eagle, and of the lion, and of the cow, man learns what he himself should utter, that utterance which today should be the good shibboleth of man's strength, and thinking, and activity:

> I must learn
> Thy power, O Cow,
> From the language
> Which the stars reveal in me.

To comprehend earth-gravity, not as mere weighing, measuring and counting; to understand not merely what lies in the physical organization of the cow, but what is embodied in her; humbly to turn our gaze away from her organization up to the heights—this alone will ensure the spiritualization of what would otherwise become the mechanistic civilization of the earth.

And the second utterance of the human being must be :

> I must learn
> Thy power, O Lion,
> From the language
> Which, through year and day,
> Encircling space makes active in me.

Notice the words "reveal", "make active".

And the third utterance which man must learn is :

> I must learn
> Thy power, O Eagle,
> From the language
> Which earth-born life creates in me.

Thus man must oppose his threefold utterance to the one-sided alluring calls, that threefold utterance whose meaning can bring what is one-sided into harmonious balance. He must learn to look towards the cow, but then, after entering with deep experience into her nature, turn his gaze upwards to what is revealed by the language of the stars. He must learn to direct his gaze upwards to the eagle, but then, after deeply experiencing within himself the eagle's nature, he must look down with the clear gaze that the eagle's nature has bestowed upon him, and behold what springs and sprouts forth from the earth, and what also works from below upwards in the organization of man. And he must learn so to behold the lion that the lion reveals to him what is wafted around him in the wind, what flashes towards him in the lightning, what rumbles around him in the thunder, what wind and weather, in the course of the seasons, bring about in the life of the earth into which man himself is yoked. Thus, when man shall direct his physical gaze upwards with his spiritual gaze downwards, when he shall direct his physical gaze downwards with his spiritual gaze upwards, when he shall direct his physical gaze outwards towards the east with

his spiritual gaze in the opposite direction towards the west—
thus when man shall allow above and below, forwards and
backwards, spiritual gaze and physical gaze to interpenetrate
each other, then he will be able to receive and understand
the true calls, bringing him strength and not weakness—the
calls of the eagle from the heights, of the lion from the
circumference, of the cow from below within the earth.

This is what man should learn in regard to his connection
with the universe, so that thereby he may become ever more
fitted to work for earth-civilization, and to serve, not its
decadence, but its upward progress.

> Learn to know my nature!
> I give thee the power
> To create a universe
> In thine own head.
>
> > Thus speaks the Eagle.
> > *West.*

> Learn to know my nature!
> I give thee the power
> To embody the universe
> In the radiance of the encircling air.
>
> > Thus speaks the Lion.
> > *Centre.*

> Learn to know my nature!
> I give thee the power
> To wrest from the universe
> Measure, number and weight.
>
> > Thus speaks the Cow.
> > *Orient.*

> I must learn
> Thy power, O Cow,
> From the language
> Which the stars reveal in me.

I must learn
Thy power, O Lion,
From the language
Which, through year and day,
Encircling space makes active in me.

I must learn
Thy power, O Eagle,
From the language
Which earth-born life creates in me.

LECTURE III

21st October, 1923

We have tried, again from a particular aspect, to place the human being into the universe. Today we wish to put the subject forward in a way which will, as it were, weld everything into a whole. During our physical life we live upon the earth; we are surrounded by those events and facts which are there because of the physical matter of the earth. This matter is moulded and shaped in the most varied manner so as to be adapted to the beings of the kingdoms of nature, up to the human form itself. The essential element in all this is the physical matter of the earth. Today—because we shall immediately have to speak about its opposite—let us call this matter the physical substance of the earth, comprising all that provides the material basis for the various earthly forms; and then let us differentiate from it everything in the universe which is the opposite of this physical substance, namely spiritual substance. This last is the basis not only of our own soul, but also of all those formations in the universe which, as spiritual formations, are connected with physical formations.

It is not right to speak only of physical matter or physical substance. Think only of the fact that we must place into the total picture of the world the beings of the higher hierarchies. These beings of the higher hierarchies have no earthly substance, no physical substance, in what in their case we would call their bodily nature. What they have is spiritual substance. When we look upon what is earthly, we become aware of physical substance; when we can look upon what is outside the earthly, we become aware of spiritual substance.

Today people know little of spiritual substance. That is why they also speak of that earth-being, who belongs both to the physical and the spiritual—the human being—as though he, too, only possessed physical substance. This, however, is not the case. Man bears both spiritual and physical substance in himself in so remarkable a way as to astonish anyone who is not accustomed to pay heed to such matters. If, for example, we consider that element in man which leads him into movement, namely what is connected with the human limb-system and its continuation inwards as digestive activity, then it is incorrect to speak primarily of physical substance. You will soon understand this still more exactly. We only speak correctly about the human being when we regard the so-called lower part of his nature as having as its basis what is in fact spiritual substance. So that, if we were to represent the human being schematically, we would have to say: The lower man actually shows us a formation in spiritual substance, and the more nearly we approach the human head, the more is man formed of physical substance. Basically the head is formed out of physical substance; but of the legs—grotesque though this may sound—it must be said that essentially they are formed of spiritual substance. So that, when we approach the head, we must represent the human being in such a way that we allow spiritual substance to pass over into physical substance; in the human head where in particular physical substance is contained. Spiritual substance, on the other hand, is diffused in a particularly beautiful way just where—if I may put it so—man stretches out his legs, stretches out his arms, into space. It is really as though the most important matter for arm and leg is precisely this being filled with spiritual substance, as if this is their essence. In the case of arm and leg it is really as though the physical substance were only swimming in the spiritual substance, whereas the head presents a compact formation composed of physical substance. In a form such as man possesses, however, we must differentiate not only the *substance,* but also *the forces.* And here again we must distinguish between spiritual forces and earthly, physical forces.

In the case of the forces, things are completely reversed. Whereas for the limb-system and digestion the substance is spiritual, the forces in the limbs, for instance in the legs, are heavy, physical forces. And whereas the substance of the head is physical, the forces active within it are spiritual. Spiritual forces play through the head; physical forces play through the spiritual substance of the limb and metabolic system in man. The human being can only be fully understood when we distinguish in him the upper region, his head and also the upper part of the breast, which are actually physical substance worked through by spiritual forces (I must mention that the lowest spiritual forces are active in the breathing). And we must regard the lower part of man as a formation composed of spiritual substance, within which physical forces are working. Only we must be clear as to how these things are interrelated in man, for the human being also projects his head-nature into his whole organism, so that the head— which is what it is because it is composed of physical substance worked through by spiritual forces—the head also projects its entire nature into the lower part of the human being; and what man is because of his spiritual substance, in which physical forces are at work, this, on the other hand, plays upwards into the upper part of the organism. In these activities in the human being there is mutual interaction. Man can in fact only be understood when he is regarded in this way, as composed of physical-spiritual substantiality and physical-spiritual dynamics, that is to say what is of the nature of forces.

This is something of great significance. For if we look away from external phenomena, and enter into the inner being, it becomes clear to us, for instance, that no irregularities can be allowed to enter into this apportioning of what is of the nature of substance and of forces in the human being.

If, for example, what should be pure substance, pure spiritual substance in man, is too strongly penetrated by physical matter, by physical substance—if, that is to say, physical substance which should in fact tend upwards towards the head makes itself too strongly felt in the metabolism— then digestion becomes too strongly affected by the head-system, and man becomes ill; certain quite definite types of illness then arise. And then the task of healing consists in paralyzing, in driving out, the physical substance-formation which is intruding into the spiritual substantiality. On the other hand, when man's digestive system, in its peculiar manner of being worked through by physical forces in spiritual substance, when this digestive system is sent up towards the head, then the head becomes, as it were, too strongly spiritualized, then there sets in a too strong spiritualization of the head. And now, because this also presents a condition of illness, care must be taken to send enough physical forces of nourishment to the head, so that they reach the head in such a way that they do not become spiritualized.

Anyone who turns his attention to man in health and sickness will very soon be able to perceive the usefulness of this differentiation, if he is really concerned with truth, and not with external illusion. But something essentially different also plays into this matter. What here plays in—the fact that man feels himself as a being constituted in the way I have described—this at first remains for the ordinary consciousness of today below in the unconscious. There, certainly, it is already present; and there it emerges as a kind of mood, a kind of life-mood of man. But it is spiritual vision alone that brings it to full consciousness, and I can only describe this spiritual vision to you thus: The man who knows from present-day initiation-science this secret of the human being, namely that the head is the most important, the most essential organ which needs physical substance with spiritual forces; who knows further that the most essential thing in the system of limbs and metabolism is spiritual substance which needs physical forces—the forces of gravity, of balance, and the other physical forces—in order to exist; who can thus penetrate with spiritual vision into this secret of the human being and who then turns his gaze back to this human, earthly existence—this man must acknowledge himself as a tremendous debtor to the world. For he must admit that in order to maintain his human existence he requires certain conditions; but through these very conditions he becomes a debtor to the earth. He is continually withdrawing something from the earth. And he finds himself obliged to say that the spiritual substance, which as man he bears within himself during earthly existence, is actually needed by the earth. When man passes through death, he should in fact leave this spiritual substance behind him for the earth, for the earth continually needs spiritual substance for its renewal. But this man cannot do, for he would then be unable to traverse his human path through the period after death. He must take this spiritual substance with him for the life between death and a new birth; he needs it, for he would disappear, so to speak, after death, if he did not take this spiritual substance with him.

Only by carrying this spiritual substance of his limb-metabolic system through the gate of death can man undergo those transformations which he must there undergo. He would be unable to meet his future incarnations if he were to give back to the earth this spiritual substance which he actually owes to it. He cannot do this. He remains a debtor. And this is something which there is no means of bettering as long as the earth remains in its middle period. At the end of earth-existence things will be otherwise.

It is indeed the case, my dear friends, that one who beholds life with spiritual vision has not only those sufferings and sorrows—perhaps also that happiness and joy—which are offered by ordinary life, but, with the beholding of the spiritual, cosmic feelings, cosmic sufferings and joys, make their appearance. And initiation is inseparable from the appearance of such cosmic suffering as, for example, the fact that one has to admit: Simply because I must maintain my humanity I must make of myself a debtor to the earth. I cannot give to the earth what I really should give if, in a cosmic sense, I were to act with complete rectitude.

Matters are similar as regards the substance which is present in the head. Because throughout the entire course of earth-life spiritual forces are working in the physical substance of the head, this head-substance becomes estranged from the earth. Man must take away from the earth the substance for his head. But he must also, in order to be man, continually imbue this substance of his head with extra-terrestrial spiritual forces. And when the human being dies, this is something extremely disturbing to the earth, because it must now take back the substance of the human head which has become so foreign to it. When the human being passes through the gate of death and yields up his head-substance to the earth, then this head-substance—which is entirely spiritualized, which bears within itself what results from the spiritual—does in fact act as a poison, as a really disturbing element, in the totality of the life of the earth. When man sees into the truth of these matters, he is obliged to say to himself that the honest thing would be to take this substance with him through the gate of death, for it would in fact be much better suited to the spiritual region which man traverses between death and a new birth. He cannot do this. For if man were to take this spiritualized earth-substance with him, he would continually create something adverse to all his development between death and a new birth. It would be the most terrible thing that could happen to man if he were to take this spiritualized head-substance with him. It would work incessantly upon the negation of his spiritual development between death and rebirth.

One must therefore acknowledge, when one sees into the truth of these things, that here, too, man becomes a debtor to the earth; for something for which he is indebted to the earth but has made useless for it, this he must continually leave behind, he cannot take it with him. What man should leave for the earth he takes from it; what man should take with him, what he has made useless for it, this man gives over to the earth with his earthly dust, thus causing the earth immense suffering in its entire life, in its whole collective being.

It is indeed the case that at first, just through spiritual

vision, something weighs heavily upon the human soul, something like a tremendous feeling of tragedy. And only when
one surveys wider epochs of time, when one beholds the development of entire systems, only then is the prospect revealed
that, when the earth will have approached its end, in later
stages of human evolution—in the Jupiter, Venus, Vulcan
stages—will man be able to restore the balance, to annul the
debt.

Thus it is not only by passing through the experiences of
a single life that man fashions karma, but man creates karma,
world karma, cosmic karma, just through the fact that he is
an earthly human being, that he is an inhabitant of the earth,
and draws his substance from the earth.

Here it is possible to look away from man, to look towards
the rest of nature and see how—though man must burden
himself with the debt of which I have just told you—balance
is nevertheless continually restored by cosmic beings. And
here one penetrates into wonderful secrets of existence, into
secrets which, when taken in conjunction with each other,
become something from which one can first gain a conception
of the wisdom of the world.

Let us turn our gaze away from man and towards something which has claimed much of our attention during the
last few days, let us turn our gaze to the world of the birds,
represented for us by the eagle. We spoke of the eagle as the
representative of the bird-world, as the creature which syn-
thesizes the characteristics and forces of the bird-kingdom.
When we consider the eagle, we are in fact considering, in
their cosmic connection, all the attributes which prevail in
the bird-world as a whole. In future, therefore, I shall simply
speak of "the eagle".

I have told you how the eagle actually corresponds to the
head of man, and how those forces which give rise to thoughts
in the human head give rise in the eagle to his plumage. So
that the sun-irradiated forces of the air, the light-imbued
forces of the air, are actually working in the eagle's plumage.

This is what shimmers in the eagle's plumage—the light-irradiated power of the air.

Now the eagle—to whom many bad qualities may certainly be ascribed—does nevertheless possess, as regards his cosmic being, the remarkable attribute that outside his skin, in the structure of his plumage, everything is retained which is formed in it by the sun-irradiated forces of the air. What takes place here is, in fact, only to be noticed when the eagle dies.

For it is only when the eagle dies that one becomes aware of what a remarkable superficial digestion he has compared with the thorough-going digestion of the cow, with its process of chewing the cud. The cow is really the animal of digestion—again as representative of many creatures of the animal kingdom. Here digestion is thoroughly performed. The eagle, like all birds, digests in a superficial way; the business of digestion is only begun. In the eagle, compared with his whole existence, digestion is merely a subsidiary process and is treated as such. On the other hand, everything in the eagle which has to do with plumage proceeds in a thorough way. (In the case of some other birds this is even more so.) Everything to do with the feathers is worked out with immense care. Such a feather is indeed a wonderful structure. Here we find most strongly in evidence what may be called earthly matter, which the eagle has taken from the earth, spiritualized by the forces of the heights, but in such a way that the eagle does not assimilate it; for the eagle makes no claim to reincarnation. He need not, therefore, be troubled about what is being brought about in the earthly matter of his plumage through the spiritual forces of the heights; he need not be troubled about how this works on in the spiritual world.

Now, when the eagle dies and his feathers fall into decay—as already mentioned this holds good for every bird—the spiritualized earthly matter ascends into spirit-land and becomes changed back into spiritual substance.

You see we have a remarkable relative interplay as regards the relationship of our head to the eagle. What we cannot do, the eagle can; he can continually conjure forth from the earth what becomes spiritualized in the earth through spiritual forces working on earthly substance.

This, too, is why we experience such a remarkable sensation when we observe an eagle in its flight. We feel him as something foreign to the earth, something which has more to do with the heavens than with the earth, although he draws his substance from the earth. But how does he do this? He obtains his substance in such a way that, as regards the earth, he is just a robber. For according to what may be called the ordinary, commonplace law of earth-existence no provision was made for the eagle to get anything. He becomes a robber; he steals his substance, as is done in all sorts of ways by the bird-kingdom as a whole. But the eagle restores the balance. He steals his material substance, but allows it to be spiritualized by the forces which exist as spiritual forces in the upper regions; and after death he carries off into spirit-land those spiritualized earth-forces which he has stolen. With the eagles the spiritualized earth-matter withdraws into spirit-land.

Now the life of animals also does not come to an end when they die. They have their significance in the universe. And the eagle in flight is only a symbol of his real being. He flies as physical eagle—Oh, but he flies further after his death! The spiritualized physical matter of the eagle nature flies into the universe in order to unite itself with the spiritual substance of spirit-land.

You see what wonderful secrets of the universe one comes upon when one enters into the reality of these things. Only then does one really learn why the various animal and other forms of the earth are there. They all have their great, their immense significance in the whole universe.

And now let us turn to the other extreme, to something which we have also studied during these days, let us turn to the cow, so venerated by the Hindu. There we have the opposite extreme. Just as the eagle is very similar to the head, so is the cow very similar to the human digestive system. The cow is the animal of digestion. And, strange as it sounds, this animal of digestion consists essentially of spiritual substance into which the physical matter consumed is merely scattered and diffused. In the cow is the spiritual substance and everywhere the physical substance penetrates into it, and is absorbed, made use of by the spiritual substance. It is in order that this may happen in a really thorough way that the process of digestion in the cow is so comprehensive, so fundamental. It is really the most fundamental digestive process that can be conceived, and in this respect—if I may put it so—the cow fosters what is fundamental to animal nature more thoroughly than any other animal in the absolute sense. She actually brings animal-nature—this animal egoism, this animal egoity—out of the universe down on to the earth, down into the region of earth-gravity.

No other animal has the same proportion between the blood-weight and the entire body-weight as the cow; other animals have either less or more blood than the cow in proportion to the weight of the body. And weight has to do with gravity and the blood with egoity; not with the ego, for this is only possessed by man, but with egoity, with separate existence. The blood also makes the animal, animal—the higher animal at least. And I must say that the cow has solved the world-problem as to the right proportion between the weight of the blood and the weight of the whole body— when there is the wish to be as thoroughly animal as possible.

You see, it was not for nothing that the ancients called the zodiac "the animal circle". The zodiac is twelvefold; it divides its totality into twelve separate parts. Those forces, which come out of the cosmos, from the zodiac, take on form and shape in the animals. But the other animals do not conform to the zodiacal proportion so exactly. The cow has a twelfth part of her body-weight in the weight of her blood. With the cow the blood-weight is a twelfth part of the body-weight; with the donkey only the twenty-third part; with the dog the tenth part. All the other animals have a different proportion. In the case of man the blood is a thirteenth of the body-weight.

You see, the cow has seen to it that, in her weight, she is

the expression of animal nature as such, that she is as thoroughly as possible the expression of what is cosmic. A fact I have mentioned repeatedly during these days—namely that one sees from the astral body of the cow that she actually manifests something lofty in physical-material substance—this comes to expression of itself through the fact that the cow maintains the partition into twelve in her own inner relationships of weight. The cosmic in her is at work. Everything to do with the cow is of such a nature that the forces of the earth are working into spiritual substance. In the cow earth-heaviness is obliged to distribute itself according to zodiacal proportion. Earth-heaviness must accommodate itself to allow a twelfth part of itself to fall away into egoity. What the cow possesses as spiritual substance has necessarily to enter into earthly conditions.

Thus the cow, lying in the meadow, is in actual fact spiritual substance, which earth-matter takes up, absorbs, makes similar to itself.

When the cow dies, this spiritual substance which the cow bears within herself can be taken up by the earth, together with the earthly matter, for the well-being of the life of the whole earth. And man is right when he feels in regard to the cow: You are the true beast of sacrifice, for you continually give to the earth what it needs, without which it could not continue to exist, without which it would harden and dry up. You continually give spiritual substance to the earth, and renew the inner mobility, the inner living activity of the earth.

When you behold on the one hand the meadow with its cattle, and on the other hand the eagle in flight, then you have their remarkable contrast: the eagle who, when he dies, carries away into the expanses of spirit-land that earth-matter, which—because it is spiritualized—has become useless for the earth; and the cow, who, when she dies, gives to the earth heavenly matter and thus renews the earth. The eagle takes from the earth what it can no longer use, what must return into spirit-land. The cow carries into the earth what the earth continually needs as renewing forces from spirit-land.

Here you become aware of something like an upsurging of feelings and perceptions from out of initiation-science. It is usually believed about this initiation-science, well, that one certainly studies it, but that it results in nothing but concepts, ideas. One fills one's head with ideas about the supersensible, just as one otherwise fills one's head with ideas about the things of the senses. But this is not how it is. Penetrating ever further into this initiation-science, we reach the point of drawing forth from the depths of the soul feelings and perceptions, the existence of which we formerly did not even surmise, but which nevertheless are there unconsciously in every human being; we reach the point of experiencing all existence differently from the way we experienced it before. And so I can describe to you an experience which actually belongs to the living comprehension of spiritual science, of initiation science. It is an experience which would make us acknowledge that if man alone were upon the earth, we should—if we recognize his true nature—have to despair of the earth ever receiving what it needs, namely, that at the right time spiritualized matter should be withdrawn and spirit-substance bestowed. We should have to experience an opposition between man and the being of the earth, which causes great, great pain, and causes that pain because we have to admit that, if man is to be rightly man upon the earth, the earth cannot be rightly earth because of man. Man and earth have need of each other, but man and earth cannot mutually support each other. What the being of the one requires is lost to the other; what the other needs is lost to the one. And we should have no security as regards the life-relationship between man and earth, were it not that the surrounding world enables us to say: What the human being is unable to achieve as regards the carrying of spiritualized earth-substance over into spirit-land, this is accomplished by the bird-kingdom; and what man is unable to do as regards giving spiritual substance to the earth, this is accomplished by the animals which chew the cud, as represented by the cow.

In this way, you see, the world is rounded into a whole. If we look only at man, uncertainty enters our feelings as regards the being of the earth; if we look at what surrounds man our feeling of certainty is restored.

And now you will wonder even less that a religious world-conception, which penetrates so deeply into the spiritual as does Hinduism, venerates the cow, for she is the animal which continually spiritualizes the earth, which continually gives to the earth that spiritual substance which she herself takes from the cosmos. And we must learn to accept as actual reality the picture that, beneath a grazing herd of cattle, the earth below is quickened to joyful, vigorous life, that there below the elemental spirits rejoice, because they are assured of their nourishment from the cosmos through the existence of the creatures grazing above them. And we would have to make another picture of the dancing, rejoicing airy circle of the elemental spirits hovering around the eagle. Then again one would portray spiritual realities, and in the spiritual realities one would see the physical; one would see the eagle extended outwards in his aura, and playing into the aura the rejoicing of the elemental air-spirits and fire-spirits of the air.

And one would see that remarkable aura of the cow, which so strongly contradicts her earthly nature, because it is entirely cosmic; and one could see the lively merriment in the senses of the elemental earth-spirits, who are thus able to perceive what has been lost to them because they are sentenced to live out their existence in the darkness of the earth. For these spirits what here appears in the cows is sun. The elemental spirits, whose dwelling place is in the earth, cannot rejoice in the physical sun, but they can rejoice in the astral bodies of the animals which chew the cud.

Yes, my dear friends, there does indeed exist a natural history which is different from what is to be found today in books. What is actually the end and aim of the natural history found today in books?

There has just appeared the sequel to that book by Albert Schweitzer which I discussed some time ago. You may remember my article dealing with this little book on present-day conditions of civilization, which appeared some time back in "The Goetheanum".* The preface to this sequel is in fact a somewhat sorry chapter in the spiritual productions of the present day; for whereas the first booklet, which I then discussed, possessed at least a certain force and the insight to admit what our civilization lacks, this preface is a really sorry chapter. For Schweitzer here takes credit to himself for being the first to perceive that, fundamentally speaking, knowledge alone can provide absolutely nothing, and that ethics and a world-conception must be gained from somewhere other than knowledge.

Now in the first place much has been said about the boundaries of knowledge, and it is—how shall I put it?—a trifle short-sighted to believe that one has been the first to speak about the boundaries of knowledge. This has been done by the natural scientists in every possible key. So one has no need to pride oneself upon being the first to discover the colossal error.

Seen apart from this, however, the fact appears that such an excellent thinker as Schweitzer—for he is an excellent thinker as his first little volume certainly shows—has reached the conclusion that if we wish to have a world-conception, if we wish to have ethics, then we must look right away from science and knowledge, for these in fact give us nothing. Recognized science and knowledge, as put forward today in books, these aspects of science and knowledge, do not enable us—as Schweitzer says—to discover meaning in the universe. For, indeed, if one looks upon the world as these personalities do, one cannot avoid the conclusion that eagles in their flight have no purpose, apart from the fact that they can be used in making armorial crests; cows are physically useful because they give milk, and so on. But because man also is regarded only as a physical being, he only possesses physical usefulness; and all this has no meaning for the world as a whole.

* See *Das Goetheanum,* No. 47 of 1923.

If people are unwilling to go further than this, they will certainly not reach the level where a world-meaning can appear; we must pass on to what the spiritual, to what initiation-science can say to us about the world; then we shall certainly discover the meaning of the world. Then we shall find this meaning of the world as we discover wonderful mysteries in all existence—mysteries such as that which unfolds itself in connection with the dying eagle and the dying cow; and there between them the dying lion, which in his turn so holds spiritual substance and physical substance in balance within himself, through the harmony he establishes in the rhythm of breathing and of blood, that it is he who regulates, through his group-soul, how many eagles are necessary, and how many cows are necessary, to enable the correct process both upwards and downwards to take its course in the way I have described to you.

You see, the three animals, eagle, lion, ox or cow, they were created out of a wonderful intuitive knowledge. Their connection with man is imbued with feeling. For the human being, when he sees into the truth of these things, must really admit: The eagle takes from me the tasks which I myself cannot fulfil through my head; the cow takes from me the tasks which I myself cannot fulfil through my metabolism, through my limb system; the lion takes from me those tasks which I myself cannot fulfil through my rhythmic system. And thus from myself and the three animals something complete is established in the cosmos.

Thus one lives one's way into cosmic relationships. Thus one feels the deep connections in the world, and learns to know how wise are those powers which hold sway in the world of being into which man is woven, and which live and move around him.

In this way, you see how we were able to weld together into a whole the divers matters which came to our knowledge when we sought to discover man's connection with the three animal representatives about whom we have spoken in recent weeks.

Part Two

The Inner Connection
of
World-Phenomena and World-Being

Cosmic activity is indeed the greatest of artists. The cosmos fashions everything according to laws which bring the deepest satisfaction to the artistic sense.

LECTURE IV

26th October, 1923

We have studied certain aspects of the connection between earth-conditions, world-conditions, animals and man. We shall continue with these studies during the coming days. Today, however, I wish to find the transition to those wider spheres which we shall have to consider later. I should like, in the first place, to draw attention to what has already been described in my "Occult Science" as the evolution of the Earth in the cosmos—beginning with the primordial Saturn-metamorphosis of the Earth. This Saturn-condition must be thought of as already containing within itself everything belonging to our planetary system. The separate planets of our planetary system, from Saturn onwards to the Moon, were at that time still within old Saturn—which, as you know, consisted only of warmth-ether—as undifferentiated world-bodies. Saturn, which had not even attained to the density of air, but was merely warmth-ether, contained in an undifferentiated etheric condition everything which later took on independent form, becoming individualized in the separate planets.

We then distinguish as the second metamorphosis of earth-evolution, what, in a comprehensive sense, I have called the Sun-condition of the Earth. Here we have to do with the gradual formation—from the fire-globe of Saturn—of the air-globe, the light-permeated, light-irradiated, glittering air-globe, Sun.

Then we have a third metamorphosis, out of which, after the ancient conditions had been recapitulated, there took form on the one hand all that was of a Sun-nature, which at that time still comprised the earth and moon—all this is described in "Occult Science"—and on the other hand all that was already externalized, and to which Saturn in its state of separation belonged.

At the same time, however, during this period of the Moon-metamorphosis, we meet the fact that the sun separated from what was now a blend of earth and moon. I have often described how the kingdoms of nature which we know today did not then exist, how the earth did not enclose a mineral mass, but was, if I may so express myself, of the nature of horn, so that the solid constituents freed themselves, forming rock-like projections of horny substance, jutting out from the Moon-mass, which was now of the consistency of water. And then there arose the conditions of the fourth metamorphosis, which are the Earth conditions of today.

Now when we depict these four metamorphoses in their sequence, we have first the Saturn-condition, which still contained dissolved within it everything later contained in our planetary system; then we have the Sun-metamorphosis, the Moon-metamorphosis, and the Earth-metamorphosis. These four manifestations fall into pairs.

Just consider how things were during the evolution of Saturn and on into the Sun-epoch, where even then substance had only advanced to a gaseous state! Evolution takes its start from the globe of fire; the fire-globe becomes metamorphosed, densified to a globe of air, which is, however, imbued with light, glittering with light. Here we have the first part of evolution.

Then we have that part of evolution in which the Moon first plays its own role. For it is the role played by the Moon which enables it to fashion those horny rock-formations. And during the Earth-metamorphosis the moon separates off, becomes a subsidiary planet, leaving behind for the Earth the inner-earth-forces. The forces of gravity, for instance, are essentially forces which, in a physical connection, have remained behind from the Moon. The Earth would never have developed the forces of gravity had not the residue of what was contained in old Moon been left behind; the moon itself departed. The present moon is that colony in cosmic space about which I spoke to you from its spiritual aspect only a few days ago. Its substantiality is quite different from that of the earth, but it left behind in the earth what, speaking in the widest sense, may be called earth-magnetism. The forces of the earth, namely the earthly forces of gravity, the activities described as the effects of weight, these have remained over from the moon. And thus we can say: on the one hand we have (Saturn-and-Sun-condition) the essentially warm, light-irradiated metamorphosis, when the two conditions are taken together; on the other we have (Moon-and-Earth-condition) the moon-sustained, watery metamorphosis, the watery condition which evolved during the Moon-metamorphosis, and which then remained during the Earth-metamorphosis; the solid element is called forth by the forces of gravity.

These two pairs of metamorphoses differ from each other to a marked degree, and we must be clear about the fact that everything present in an earlier condition is again inherent in the later one. What constituted the ancient fire-globe of Saturn remained as warmth-substance in all the subsequent metamorphoses; and when today we move about in the regions of the earth, and everywhere encounter warmth, this warmth which is everywhere to be found is the remains of the ancient Saturn condition. Wherever we find air, or gaseous bodies, we have the remains of the ancient Sun-evolution. When, having imbued ourselves with feeling and understanding for this epoch of evolution, we look out into the sun-irradiated atmosphere, we can say to ourselves with truth: In this sun-irradiated atmosphere we have remains of the ancient Sun-evolution; for had this ancient Sun-evolution not taken place, the relationship of our air with the rays of the sun, which are now there outside, would not have existed. Only through the fact that the sun was once united with the earth, that the light of the sun itself shone in the earth which was still in a gaseous condition—so that the earth was an air-globe radiating light into cosmic space—only through this could the later metamorphosis appear, the present Earth-metamorphosis, in which the earth is enveloped by an atmosphere of air, into which the sun's rays fall from outside. But these sun-rays have a deep inner connection with the earth's atmosphere. They do not, however, behave—as present-day physicists somewhat crudely state—as though projected like small shot through the gaseous atmosphere; but the rays of the sun have a deep inner relationship with the air. And this relationship is actually the after-effect of their one-time union during the Sun-metamorphosis. Thus everything is mutually inter-related through the fact that the earlier conditions ever and again play into the later conditions in manifold ways. But during the time in which, speaking generally, earth-evolution took its course—as you find in "Occult Science", and as I have briefly sketched it for you here—everything on and around the earth, everything also within the earth, has been evolved.

And now we can say: When we contemplate the present-day earth, we have within it what produces the solid element, the inner moon, actually anchored in earth-magnetism; the inner moon, whose action is such that it is the cause of the solid-element, the cause which produces everything which has weight. And it is the forces of weight which form the solid element out of the fluid. We have next the actual earth-realm, the watery element which appears in manifold ways—as underground water, for instance, but also in the water which is present in the rising mist-formations, in the descending rain clouds, and so on. And further we have in the circumference what is of the nature of air. Moreover all this is permeated by the element of fire, the remains of old Saturn. So that we also have to ascribe to our present-day earth what, there above, is Sun-Saturn or Saturn-Sun. We can always say to ourselves: Everything which is present in the warm air, which is irradiated with light, is Saturn-Sun. We look up and actually find our air imbued with what is Saturn-activity, what is Sun-activity, evolving in the course of time into the actual atmosphere of the earth, which, however, is only an after-effect of the Sun-metamorphosis. Broadly speaking, this is what we find when we direct our gaze upwards.

When we direct our gaze downwards, it is more a question of what arose from the last two metamorphoses. We have what is heavy, the solid element, or better expressed, the working of the forces of weight into what is becoming solid; we have the fluid element, we have the Moon-Earth. These two parts of earth-existence can be strictly differentiated from each other.

If you read "Occult Science'" again with this in mind, you will see that the whole style alters at the place where the Sun-metamorphosis passes over into the Moon-metamorphosis. Even today there is still a kind of sharp contrast between what is above, what is of the nature of Saturn, and what is below, what is of the nature of Earth-Moon-watery condition.

Thus we can quite well differentiate between the Saturn-Sun-gaseous element and the Moon-Earth fluidic element.

When someone who sees into these things with initiation science contemplates the general course of earth-evolution—everything also which has developed along with the earth, which belongs to it—his gaze falls first upon the manifold variety of the insect world. One can well imagine that the very feeling engendered by the fluttering, glittering insect world would bring us into a certain connection with what is above, with what is of the nature of the Saturn-Sun-gaseous condition. And this is indeed the case. When we look at the butterfly with its shimmering colours, we see it fluttering in the air, in the light-flooded, light-irradiated air. It is upborne by the waves of the air. It hardly contacts what is of an Earth-Moon-fluid nature. Its element is in the upper regions. And when one investigates the course of earth-evolution, it is a remarkable thing that just in the case of the small insect one arrives at very early epochs of earth-metamorphosis. What today shimmers in the light-irradiated air as the butterfly's wings was first formed in germ during old Saturn, and developed further during the time of old Sun. It was then that there arose what still today makes it possible for the butterfly to be in its very nature a creation of light and air. The sun owes the gift of diffusing light to itself. The sun owes the gift that its light can call forth in substances what is fiery, shimmering, to the working-in of Saturn-Jupiter-Mars. The butterfly-nature cannot indeed be understood by one who seeks for it on the earth.

The forces active in the nature of the butterfly, must be sought above, must be sought in Sun, Mars, Jupiter, Saturn. And when we enter more exactly into this wonderful evolution of the butterfly—I have already described it, in its connection with the human being, as what may be called the cosmic embodiment of memory—when we enter into this more exactly, we find in the first place the fluttering butterfly shimmering with light, carried up above the earth by the air. It then deposits its egg. Yes, the crude materialist says: "The butterfly deposits its egg", because, under the influence of present-day unscientific science, the things of greatest importance are simply not studied. The question is this: To what does the butterfly entrust its egg when it deposits it?

Now investigate any place where the butterfly deposits its egg; everywhere you will find that the egg is deposited in such a way that it cannot be withdrawn from the influence of the sun. The sun's influence upon the earth is in fact not only present when the sun is shining directly on to the earth. I have often drawn attention to the fact that in winter peasants put their potatoes into the earth, cover them with earth, because what comes towards the earth during summer as the sun's warmth and the power of the sunlight, is, just during winter, within the earth. On the surface of the earth potatoes become frosted; they do not become frosted but remain really good potatoes if they are buried in a pit and covered with a layer of earth, because throughout the winter the activity of the sun is inside the earth. Throughout the whole winter we must look for the sun-activity of summer under the earth. In December, for example, at a certain depth within the earth, we have the July-activity of the sun. In July the sun radiates its light and warmth on to the surface. The warmth and light gradually penetrate deeper. And if in December we wish to look for what we experience in July on the surface of the earth, we must dig a pit, and then what was on the surface of the earth in July will be found in December at a certain depth within it. There the potato is buried in the July sun. Thus the sun is not only where crude materialistic understanding looks for it; the sun is actually present in many spheres. Only this is strictly regulated according to the seasons of the year in the cosmos.

The butterfly never deposits its eggs where they cannot remain in some way or other in connection with the sun. Consequently one expresses oneself badly when one says that the butterfly lays its eggs in the realm of the earth. This it does not do at all. It lays its eggs in the realm of the sun. The butterfly never descends as far down as the earth. Wherever the sun is present in what is earthly, there the butterfly seeks out the place to deposit its eggs, so that they remain entirely under the influence of the sun. In no way do they come under the influence of the earth.

Then, as you know, out of this butterfly's egg creeps the caterpillar. When it emerges, it remains under the influence of the sun, but it now comes under another influence as well. The caterpillar would be unable to crawl did it not also come under another influence. And this is the influence of Mars.

If you picture the earth with Mars circling around it, what emanates from Mars in the upper region pervades everything, and remains everywhere. It is not a question of Mars itself being anywhere in particular, but we have the whole Mars sphere, and when the caterpillar crawls in some direction, it does so in the sense of the Mars sphere. Then the caterpillar becomes a chrysalis, building around itself a cocoon. We get a cocoon. I described to you how this is a sacrifice to the sun on the part of the caterpillar, how the threads which are spun into it are spun in the direction of the line of light. The caterpillar is exposed to the sun, follows the rays of light, spins, stops when it is dark, spins on further. The whole cocoon is actually cosmic sunlight, sunlight which is interwoven with matter. Thus when you have the cocoon of the silkworm, for example—which is used to make your silk garments—what is present in the silk is actually sunlight, into which is spun the substance of the silkworm. Out of its own body the silkworm spins its matter in the direction of the sun's rays, and in this way forms the cocoon around itself. But that this may happen it needs the intervention of the Jupiter activity.

And then, as you know, the butterfly creeps out of the cocoon, out of the chrysalis—the butterfly which is upborne by light, radiant with light. It leaves the dark chamber into which the light only entered as it did into the cromlechs, in the way I described this to you, in the case of the cromlechs of the ancient Druids. The sun, however, comes under the influence of Saturn, and it is only in conjunction with Saturn that it can send its light into the air in such a way that the butterfly can shine in the radiance of its variegated colours.

And thus, when we behold that wonderful sea of fluttering butterflies in the atmosphere, we must say: That is in truth no earthly creation, but is born into the earth from above. The butterfly nowhere goes deeper with its egg than to where influences come to the earth from the sun. The cosmos bestows on the earth the sea of butterflies, Saturn bestows their colours. The sun bestows the power of flight, called forth by the sustaining power of the light, and so on.

Thus I might say that we actually have to see in the butterflies little creatures, strewn down, as it were, upon the earth by the sun, and by what is above the sun in our planetary system. The butterflies, the dragonflies, the insects in general, are actually the gift of Saturn, Jupiter, Mars and Sun. And not a single insect could be produced by the earth, not so much as a flea, were it not that the planets beyond the sun, together with the sun, bestow upon the earth the gift of insect life. And we do in truth owe the fact that Saturn, Jupiter, etc. could so generously allow the insect world to flutter in upon us to the first two metamorphoses experienced by earth-evolution.

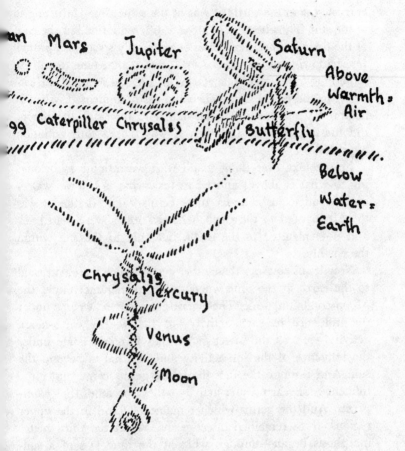

And now let us look at the way in which the two last metamorphoses—the Moon-condition and the Earth-condition—have played their part. In view of the fact that the butterfly's egg is never actually entrusted to the earth, it must be pointed out that at the time when the Moon-metamorphosis, the third condition, was in its beginning, the butterflies were not as yet as they are today. The earth, too, was not so dependent upon the sun. At the beginning of the third metamorphosis the sun was actually still united with the earth, and only later became separated. The butterfly, therefore, was not so averse to entrusting its germ to the earth. When it entrusted it to the earth, it was at the same time entrusting it to the sun. Thus here there arose a differentiation. In the case of the first two metamorphoses one can only speak of a primal foreshadowing of the insect world. But at that time to entrust something to the outer planets, to the sun, still signified entrusting it to the earth. Only when the earth condensed, when it acquired water, acquired the magnetic forces of the moon, did matters change, and then it was that a differentiation appeared.

Let us take everything to do with warmth-air as belonging to what is above; and let us take what is below : water-earth. And let us consider those germs whose destiny it was to be entrusted to the earth, whereas others were held back and not entrusted to the earth, but only to the sun within the earthly.

Now let us consider these other germs which were entrusted to the earth at the time when the third metamorphosis, the Moon-condition, arose. These germs, you see, now came under the influence of earth-activity—of the watery earth-moon activity—just as the insect germs had formerly come under the influence of the sun-activity and of what is beyond the sun. And through the fact that these germs came under the influence of earth-water-activity, they became the *plant-germs*. And the germs which remained behind in the upper regions, these remained insect-germs. When the third metamorphosis began—through what at the time was of a sun-nature becoming transformed into what was of the nature of moon-earth—the plant-germs came into being, during this third metamorphosis of earth-evolution. And what you now have in the butterfly, under the development of the extra-terrestrial cosmos, this whole development from the germ, through the caterpillar, through the chrysalis to the butterfly —this you are now in a position to follow in the plant. In that the seed became earthly it was not the butterfly which developed; but when the seed became earthly, entrusted to the earth—not now to the sun—the plant root developed, the first thing to arise out of the germ. And instead of the caterpillar creeping out, under the influence of the forces which proceed from Mars, the leaf arises, creeping upwards in spiral formation. The leaf is the caterpillar which has come under the influence of what is earthly. When you see the creeping caterpillar, you have, in the upper regions, what corresponds, below, to the leaf of the plant; the leaf develops out of what became root through the fact that the seed was transplanted from the region of the sun to the region of the earth.

Proceeding further upwards, we find contracted to the calyx what is of the nature of the chrysalis. And finally the butterfly develops in the blossom, which is coloured, just like the butterfly in the air. The circle is completed. Just as the butterfly lays its egg, so does the blossom develop within itself the new seed for the future. So you see, we look up towards the butterfly, and we understand it to be the plant raised up into the air. What the butterfly becomes from egg to full development under the influence of the sun with the upper planets, the plant becomes here below under the influence of the earth. When the plant comes into leaf (see diagram) we have from the earth-aspect the influence of the moon, then the Venus-influence and the Mercury-influence. Then there is a return to the earth-influence. The seed is again under earth-influence.

We can, therefore, place before ourselves two verses, which give expression to a great secret of nature :

> Behold the plant :
> It is the butterfly
> Fettered by the earth.

> Behold the butterfly :
> It is the plant
> Freed by the cosmos.

The plant—the butterfly fettered by the earth ! The butter-fly—the plant freed from the earth by the cosmos !*

If one looks at the butterfly, indeed at any insect, from the

* Coleridge describes the butterfly as *Flos libertus vel libertinus*. Ed.

stage of the egg to when it is fluttering away, it is the plant raised up into the air, fashioned in the air by the cosmos. If one looks at the plant, it is the butterfly fettered to what is below. The egg is claimed by the earth. The caterpillar is metamorphosed into leaf-formation. In what is contracted in the plant we have the metamorphosis of the chrysalis-formation. And then what unfolds into the butterfly itself, in the plant develops into the blossom. Small wonder that such an intimate relationship exists between the world of the butterflies, the insect-world in general, and the world of the plants. For in truth those spiritual beings which are behind the insects, the butterflies, must say to themselves: There below are our relatives; we must have intercourse with them, unite ourselves with them—unite ourselves with them in the enjoyment of their juices, and so on, for they are our brothers. They are our brothers who have wandered down into the domain of the earth, who have become fettered to the earthly, who have won another existence.

And again, the spirits who ensoul the plants can look up to the butterflies and say: These are the heavenly relatives of the earthly plants.

You see, one must really say that understanding of the world cannot come about through abstractions, for abstractions do not attain to understanding. Cosmic activity is indeed the greatest of artists. The cosmos fashions everything according to laws which bring the deepest satisfaction to the artistic sense. And no-one can understand the butterfly, which has sunk down into the earth, unless he metamorphoses abstract thoughts into artistic sense. No-one can understand the nature of the blossoming plant, which, as the butterfly, has been uplifted into the air by the light and by cosmic forces, unless once again he can bring artistic movement into abstract thoughts. Nevertheless there always remains something immensely uplifting when we turn our minds to the deep, inward connection between the things and beings of nature.

It is a unique experience to see an insect poised on a plant, and at the same time to see how the astrality holds sway above the blossom. Here the plant is striving outwards from the earthly. The plant's longing for the heavenly works and weaves above the iridescent petals of the blossom. The plant cannot of itself satisfy this longing. Thus there radiates towards it from the cosmos what is of the nature of the butter-fly. In beholding this the plant realizes the satisfaction of its own desires. And this is the wonderful relationship existing in the environment of the earth, namely that the longings of the plant-world are assuaged in looking up to the insects, in particular the world of the butterflies. What the blossoming flower longs for, as it radiates its colour out into world-space becomes for it fulfilment in knowledge when the butterfly approaches it with its shimmer of colours. Outstreaming warmth, outstreaming longing : instreaming satisfaction from the heavens—this is the interplay between the world of the blossoming plants and the world of the butterflies. This is what we should see in the environment of the earth.

Having thus established the connection with the plant-world, I shall now be in the position to extend still further in the near future the studies which lead from the human being to the animals. We can already include the plant-world, and thus we shall gradually come to man's connection with the whole earth. But for this it was necessary to build, as it were, a bridge from the fluttering plant of the air, the butterfly, to the butterfly firmly rooted in the earth, the plant. The earthly plant is the firmly rooted butterfly. The butterfly is the flying plant. Having recognized this connection be-tween the earth-bound plant and the heaven-freed butterfly, we have now established the bridge between the animal-world and the plant-world, and thus we can now look down with a certain unconcern upon all the trivialities which are always saying how spontaneous generation, and the like took place. These prosaic concepts will never lead us into those regions of the universe to which we must attain. Those spheres are only reached when prosaic concepts can be led over into artistic concepts, so that we may then arrive at the picture of how, from the heaven-born butterfly which is only entrusted to the sun, the plant later arose through this butterfly's egg becoming metamorphosed in such a way that, whereas it was formerly entrusted to the sun, it now became entrusted to the earth.

LECTURE V

27th October, 1923

These lectures deal with the inner connection between appearance and reality in the world, and you have already seen that there are many things of which those whose vision is limited to the world of appearance have no idea. We have seen how every species of being—this was shown by a number of examples—has its task in the whole nexus of cosmic existence. Now today, as a kind of recapitulation, we will again consider what I said recently about the nature of several beings and in the first place of the butterfly. In my description of this butterfly nature, as contrasted with that of the plants, we found that the butterfly is essentially a being belonging to the light—to the light in so far as it is modified by the forces of the outer planets, of Mars, of Jupiter, and of Saturn. Hence, if we wish to understand the butterfly in its true nature, we must in fact look up into the higher regions of the cosmos, and must say to ourselves : These higher cosmic regions endow and bless the earth, with the world of the butterflies.

The bestowal of this blessing upon the earth has an even deeper significance. Let us recall how we had to say that the butterfly does not participate in what is directly connected with earthly existence, but only indirectly, in so far as the sun, with its power of warmth and light, is active in this earthly existence. Actually a butterfly lays its eggs only where they do not become separated from sun activity, so that the butterfly does not entrust its egg to the earth, but only to the sun. Then out creeps the caterpillar, which is under the influence of Mars-activity, though naturally the sun influence always remains present. Then the chrysalis is formed, and this is under the influence of Jupiter-activity. Out of the chrysalis emerges the butterfly, which can now in its iridescent colours reproduce in the earth's environment the luminous Sun-power of the earth united with the power of Saturn.

Thus in the manifold colours of the butterfly world we see, in the environment of earth-existence, the direct working of Saturn-activity within the sphere of the earthly. But let us bear in mind that the substances necessary for earth-existence are in fact of two kinds. We have the purely material substances of the earth, and we have the spiritual substances; and I told you that the remarkable thing about this is that in the case of man the underlying substance of his metabolic and limb system is spiritual whereas that of the head is physical. Moreover in man's lower nature spiritual substance is permeated with the activity of physical forces, with the action of gravity, with the action of the other earthly forces. In the head, the earthly substance, conjured up into it by the whole digestive process, the circulation, nerve-activity and the like, is permeated by super-sensible spiritual forces, which are reflected in our thinking, in our power of forming mental pictures. Thus in the human head we have spiritualized physical matter, and in the metabolic-limb-system we have earthized—if I may coin a word—earthized spiritual substantiality.

Now it is this spiritualized matter that we find to the greatest degree in the butterfly. Because a butterfly always remains in the sphere of sun-existence, it only takes to itself earthly matter—naturally I am still speaking pictorially—as though in the form of the finest dust. It also derives its nourishment from those earthly substances which are worked upon by the sun. It unites with its own being only what is sun-imbued; and it takes from earthly substance only what is finest, and works on it until it is entirely spiritualized. When we look at a butterfly's wing we actually have before us earthly matter in its most spiritualized form. Through the fact that the matter of the butterfly's wing is imbued with colour, it is the most spiritualized of all earthly substances.

The butterfly is the creature which lives entirely in spiritualized earth-matter. And one can even see spiritually how in a certain way a butterfly despises the body which it carries between its coloured wings, because its whole attention, its whole group-soul being, is centred on its joyous delight in the colours of its wings.

And just as we marvel at its shimmering colours as we follow it, so also can we marvel at its own fluttering joy in these colours. This is something which it is of fundamental importance to cultivate in children, this joy in the spirituality fluttering about in the air, which is in fact fluttering joy, joy in the play of colours. The nuances of butterfly-nature reflect all this in a wonderful way : and something else lies in the background as well.

We were able to say of the bird—which we regarded as represented by the eagle—that at its death it can carry spiritualized earth-substance into the spiritual world, and that thereby, as bird, it has the task in cosmic existence of spiritualizing earthly matter, thus being able to accomplish what cannot be done by man. The human being also possesses in his head earth-matter which has been to a certain degree spiritualized, but he cannot take this earthly matter into the world in which he lives between death and a new birth, for he would continually have to endure unspeakable, unbearable, devastating pain, if he were to carry this spiritualized earth-matter of his head into the spiritual world.

The bird-world, represented by the eagle, can do this, so that thereby a connection is actually created between what is earthly and what is extra-earthly. Earthly matter is, as it were, gradually converted into spirit, and the bird-creation has the task of giving over this spiritualized earthly matter to the universe. One can actually say that, when the earth has reached the end of its existence, this earth-matter will have been spiritualized, and that the bird-creation had its place in the whole economy of earthly existence for the purpose of carrying back this spiritualized earth-matter into spirit-land.

It is somewhat different with butterflies. The butterfly spiritualizes earthly matter to an even greater degree than the bird. The bird after all comes into much closer contact with the earth than does the butterfly. I will explain this in detail later. Because the butterfly never actually leaves the region of the sun, it is in a position to spiritualize its matter to such a degree that it does not, like the bird, have to await its death, but already during its life it is continually restoring spiritualized matter to the environment of the earth, to the cosmic environment of the earth.

Only think of the magnificence of all this in the whole cosmic economy! Only picture the earth with the world of the butterflies fluttering around it in its infinite variety, continually sending out into world-space the spiritualized earthly matter which this butterfly-world yields up to the cosmos! Then, with such knowledge, we can contemplate the region of the world, of the butterflies encircling the earth with totally different feelings.

We can look into this fluttering world and say: From you, O fluttering creatures, there streams out something still better than sunlight; you radiate spirit-light into the cosmos! Our materialistic science pays but little heed to things of the spirit. And so this materialistic science is absolutely unequipped with any means of grasping at these things, which are, nevertheless, part of the whole cosmic economy. They are there, just as the effects of physical activities are there, and they are even more real. For what thus streams out into spirit-land will work on further when the earth has long passed away, whereas what is taught by the modern chemist and physicist will reach its end with the conclusion of the earth's existence. So that if some observer or other were to sit outside in the cosmos, with a long period of time for observation, he would see something like a continual outstreaming into spirit-land of matter which has become spiritualized, as the earth radiates its own being out into cosmic space; and he would see—like scintillating sparks, sparks which ever and again flash up into light—what the bird-kingdom, what every bird after its death sends forth as glittering light, streaming out into the universe in the form of rays: a shimmering of

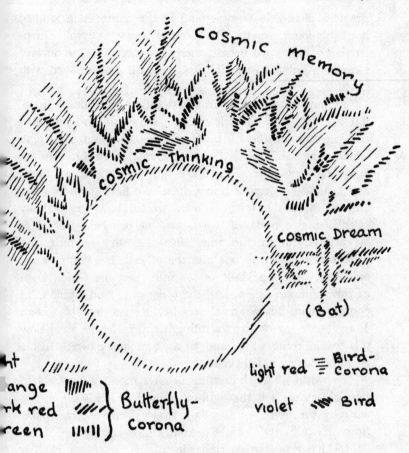

cosmic memory

cosmic Thinking

cosmic Dream

(Bat)

light red ☰ Bird-Corona

violet ➤ Bird

ht /////////
ange //////
rk red ////
een ///// } Butterfly-Corona

the spirit-light of the butterflies, and a sparkling of the spirit-light of the birds.

Such things as these should also make us realize that, when we look up to the rest of the starry world, we should not think that from there, too, there only streams down what is shown by the spectroscope, or rather what is conjured into the spectroscope by the fantasy of the expert in optics. What streams down to earth from other worlds of the stars is just as much the product of living beings in other worlds, as what streams out from the earth into world-space is the product of living beings. People look at a star, and with the modern physicist picture it as something in the nature of a kindled inorganic flame—or the like. This, of course, is absolute non-sense. For what we behold there is entirely the product of something imbued with life, imbued with soul, imbued with spirit.

And now let us pass inwards from this girdle of butterflies—if I may call it so—which encircles the earth, and return to the kingdom of the birds. If we call to mind something which is already known to us, we must picture three regions adjoining each other. There are other regions above these, and again other regions below them. We have the light-ether and we have the warmth-ether, which, however, actually consists of two parts, of two layers, the one being the layer of earthly warmth, the other that of cosmic warmth, and these continually play one into the other. Thus we have not only one, but two kinds of warmth, the one which is of earthly, tellurian origin, and the other of a kind which is of cosmic origin. These are always playing one into the other. Then, bordering on the warmth-ether, there is the air. Below this would come water and earth, and above would come chemical ether and light-ether.

The world of the butterflies belongs more particularly to the light-ether; it is the light-ether itself which is the means whereby the power of the light draws forth the caterpillar from the butterfly's egg. Essentially it is the power of the light which draws the caterpillar forth.

This is not the case with the bird-kingdom. The birds lay their eggs. These must now be hatched out by warmth. The butterfly's egg is simply given over to what is of the nature of the sun; the bird's egg comes into the region of warmth. It is in the region of the warmth-ether that the bird has its being, and it overcomes what is purely of the air.

The butterfly, too, flies in the air, but fundamentally it is entirely a creature of the light. And in that the air is per-meated with light, in this light-air existence, the butterfly chooses not air existence but light existence. For the butterfly the air is only what sustains it—the waves, as it were, upon which it floats; but the butterfly's element is the light. The bird flies in the air, but its element is the warmth, the various differentiations of warmth in the air, and to a certain degree it overcomes the air. Certainly the bird is also an air-being inwardly and to a high degree. The bones of the mammals, the bones of the human being are filled with marrow. (We shall speak later as to why this is the case.) The bones of a bird are hollow and are filled only with air. We consist, in so far as the content of our bones is concerned, of what is of the nature of marrow; a bird consists of air. And what is of the nature of marrow in us for the bird is simply air. If you take the lungs of a bird, you will find a whole quantity of pockets which project from the lungs; these are air-pockets. When the bird inhales it does not only breathe air into its lungs, but it breathes the air into these air-pockets, and from thence it passes into the hollow bones. So that, if one could remove from the bird all its flesh and all its feathers and also take away the bones, one would still get a creature composed of air, having the form of what inwardly fills out the lungs, and what inwardly fills out all the bones. Picturing this in accordance with its form, you would really get the form of the bird. Within the eagle of flesh and bone dwells an eagle of air. This is not only because within the eagle there is also an eagle of air. The bird breathes and through its breathing it produces warmth. This warmth the bird imparts to the air, and draws it into its entire limb system. Thus arises the difference of temperature as compared to its outer environment. The bird has its inner warmth, as against the outer warmth. In this difference of degree between the warmth of the outer air and the warmth which the bird imparts to its own air within itself—it is really in this that the bird lives and has its being. And if you were to ask a bird how matters are with its body—supposing you understood bird language—the bird's reply would make you realize that it regards its solid material bones, and other material adjuncts, rather as you would luggage if you were loaded, left and right, on the back and on the head. You would not call this luggage your body. In the same way the bird, in speaking of itself, would only speak of the warmth-imbued air, and of everything else as the luggage which it bears about with it in earthly existence. These bones, which envelop the real body of the bird, these are its luggage. We are therefore, speaking in an absolute sense when we say that fundamentally the bird lives only and entirely in the element of warmth, and the butterfly in the element of light. For the butterfly everything of the nature of physical substance, which it spiritualizes, is, before this spiritualizing, not even personal luggage but more like furniture. It is even more remote from its real being.

When we thus ascend to the creatures of these regions, we come to something which cannot be judged in a physical way. If we do so, it is rather as if we were to draw a person with his hair growing out of the bundle on his head, boxes growing together with his arms, and a rucksack growing out of his back, making him appear a perfect hunch-back. If one were to draw a person in this way, it would actually correspond to the materialist's view of the bird. That is not the bird; it is the bird's luggage. The bird really feels encumbered by having to drag his luggage about, for it would like best to pursue its way through the world, free and unencumbered, as a creature of warm air. For the bird all else is a burden. And the bird pays tribute to world-existence by spiritualizing this burden for it, sending it out when it dies into spirit-land; a tribute which the butterfly already pays during its lifetime.

You see, the bird breathes, and makes use of the air in the way I told you. It is otherwise with the butterfly. The butterfly does not in any way breathe by means of an apparatus such as the so-called higher animals possess—though these in fact are only the more bulky, not in reality the higher animals. The butterfly breathes in fact only through tubes which proceed inwards from its outer casing, and, these being somewhat dilated, it can accumulate air during flight, so that it is not inconvenienced by always needing to breathe.

The butterfly always breathes through tubes which pass into its interior. Because this is so, it can take up into its whole body, together with the air which it inhales, the light which is in the air. Here, too, a great difference is to be found.

Let us represent this in a diagram. Picture to yourselves one of the higher animals, one with lungs. Into the lungs comes oxygen, and there it unites with the blood in its course through the heart. In the case of these bulky animals, and also with man, the blood must flow into the heart and lungs in order to come into contact with oxygen.

In the case of the butterfly I must draw the diagram quite differently. Here I must draw it in this way : If this is the butterfly, the tubes everywhere pass inwards; they then branch out more widely. And now the oxygen enters in everywhere, and spreads itself out through the tubes; so that the air penetrates into the whole body.

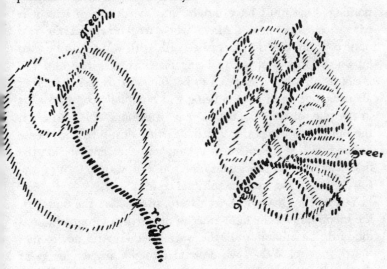

With us, and with the so-called higher animals, the air comes as far as the lungs *as air only*; in the case of the butterfly the outer air, *with its content of light,* is dispersed into the whole interior of the body. The bird diffuses the air right into its hollow bones; the butterfly is not only a creature of light outwardly, but it diffuses the light which is carried by the air into every part of its entire body, so that inwardly too the butterfly is composed of light. Just as I could characterize the bird as warmed air, so in fact is the butterfly composed entirely of light. Its body also consists of light; and for the butterfly warmth is actually a burden, is luggage. It flutters about only and entirely in the light, and it is light only that it builds into its body. When we see the butterflies fluttering in the air, what we must really see is only fluttering beings of light, beings of light rejoicing in their play of colours. All else is garment, is luggage. We must gain an understanding of what the beings around earth really consist, for outward appearance is deceptive.

Those who today have learned, in some superficial manner, this or that out of oriental wisdom speak about the world as Maya. But to say that the world is Maya really implies nothing. One must have insight into the details of why it is Maya. We understand Maya when we know that the real nature of the bird in no way accords with what is to be seen outwardly, but that it is a being of warm air. The butterfly is not at all what it appears to be, but what is seen fluttering about is a being of light, a being which actually consists of joy in the play of colours, in that play of colours which arises on the butterfly's wings through the earthly dust-substance being imbued with the element of colour, and thus entering on the first stage of its spiritualization on the way out into the spiritual universe, into the spiritual cosmos.

You see, we have here, as it were, two levels: the butterfly, the inhabitant of the light-ether in an earth environment, and the bird, the inhabitant of the warmth-ether. And now comes the third level. When we descend into the air, we arrive at those beings which, at a certain period of our earth-evolution, could not yet have been there at all; for instance at the time when the moon had not yet separated from the earth but was still with it. Here we come to beings which are certainly also air-beings, living in the air, but which are in fact already strongly influenced by what is peculiar to the earth, gravity. The butterfly is completely untouched by earth-gravity. It flutters joyfully in the light-ether, and feels itself to be a creation of that ether. The bird overcomes gravity by imbuing the air within it with warmth, thereby becoming a being of warm air—and warm air is upborne by cold air. Earth-gravity is also overcome by the bird.

Those creatures which by reason of their origin must still live in the air but which are unable to overcome earth-gravity, because they have not hollow bones but bones filled with marrow, and also because they have not air-sacs like the birds—these creatures are the bats.

The bats are a quite remarkable order of animal-life. In no way do they overcome the gravity of earth through what is inside their bodies. They do not, like the butterflies, possess the lightness of light, or, like the bird, the lightness of warmth; they are subject to earth-gravity, and they experience themselves in their flesh and bone. Hence that element of which the butterfly consists, which is its whole sphere of life—the element of light—this is disagreeable to bats. They like the dusk. Bats have to make use of the air, but they like the air best when it is not the bearer of light. They yield themselves up to the dusk. They are veritable creatures of the dusk. And bats can only maintain themselves in the air because they possess their somewhat caricature-like bat-wings, which are not wings at all in the true sense, but stretched membrane, membrane stretched between their elongated fingers, a kind of parachute. By means of these they maintain themselves in the air. They overcome gravity—as a counter-weight—by opposing it with something which itself is related to gravity. Through this, however, they are completely yoked into the domain of earth-forces. One could never construct the flight of a butterfly solely according to physical, mechanical laws, neither could one the flight of a bird. Things would never come out absolutely right. In their case we must introduce something containing other laws of construction. But the bat's flight, that you can certainly construct according to earthly dynamics and mechanics.

The bat does not like the light, the light-imbued air, but at the most only twilight air. And the bat also differs from the bird through the fact that the bird, when it looks about it, always has in view what is in the air. Even the vulture, when it steals a lamb, perceives it as it sees it from above, as though it were at the end of the light sphere, like something painted on to the earth. And quite apart from this, it is no mere act of seeing; it is a craving. What you would perceive if you actually saw the flight of the vulture towards the lamb is a veritable dynamic of intention, of volition, of craving.

A butterfly sees what is on the earth as though in a mirror; for the butterfly the earth is a mirror. It sees what is in the cosmos. When you see a butterfly fluttering about, you must picture to yourselves that it disregards the earth, that for it the earth is just a mirror for what is in the cosmos. A bird does not see what belongs to the earth, but it sees what is in the air. The bat only perceives what it flies through, or flies past. And because it does not like the light, it is unpleasantly affected by everything it sees. It can certainly be said that the butterfly and the bird see in a very spiritual way. The first creature—descending from above downwards—which must see in an earthly way, is disagreeably affected by this seeing. A bat dislikes seeing, and in consequence it has a kind of embodied fear of what it sees, but does not want to see. And so it would like to slip past everything. It is obliged to see, yet is unwilling to do so—and thus it everywhere tries just to skirt past. And it is because it desires just to slip past everything, that it is so wonderfully intent on listening. The bat is actually a creature which is continually listening to its own flight, lest this flight should be in any way endangered.

Only look at the bat's ears. You can see from them that they are attuned to world-fear. So they are—these bats' ears. They are quite remarkable structures, attuned to evading the world, to world-fear. All this, you see, is only to be understood when the bat is studied in the framework into which we have just placed it.

Here we must add something further. The butterfly continually imparts spiritualized matter to the cosmos. It is the darling of the Saturn influences. Now call to mind how I described Saturn as the great bearer of the memory of our planetary system. The butterfly is closely connected with what makes provision for memory in our planet. It is memory-thoughts which live in the butterfly. The bird—this, too, I have already described—is entirely a head, and as it flies through the warmth-imbued air in world-space it is actually the living, flying thought. What we have within us as thoughts —and this also is connected with the warmth-ether—is bird-nature, eagle-nature, in us. The bird is the flying thought. But the bat is the flying dream; the flying dream-picture of the cosmos. So we can say: The earth is surrounded by a web of butterflies—this is cosmic memory; and by the king-dom of the birds—this is cosmic thinking; and by the bats—they are the cosmic dream, cosmic dreaming. It is actually the flying dreams of the cosmos which sough through space as the bats. And as dreams love the twilight, so, too, does the cosmos love the twilight when it sends the bat through space. The enduring thoughts of memory, these we see embodied in the girdle of butterflies encircling the earth; thoughts of the moment we see in the bird-girdle of the earth; and dreams in the environment of the earth fly about embodied as bats. And you will surely feel, if we penetrate deeply into their form, how much affinity there is between this appearance of the bat and dreaming! One simply cannot look at a bat without the thought arising: I must be dreaming; that is really something which should not be there, something which is as much outside the other creations of nature as dreams are outside ordinary physical reality.

To sum up we can say: The butterfly sends spiritualized substance into spirit-land during its lifetime; the bird sends it out after its death. Now what does the bat do? During its lifetime the bat gives off spiritualized substance, especially that spiritualized substance which exists in the stretched membrane between its separate fingers. But it does not give this over to the cosmos; it sheds it into the atmosphere of the earth. Thereby beads of spirit, so to say, are continually arising in the atmosphere.

Thus we find the earth to be surrounded by the continual glimmer of outstreaming spirit-matter from the butterflies, and sparkling into this what comes from the dying birds; but also, streaming back towards the earth, we find peculiar segregations of air where the bats give off what they spiritualize. Those are the spiritual formations which are always to be observed when one sees a bat in flight. In fact a bat always has a kind of tail behind it, like a comet. The bat gives off spirit-matter; but instead of sending it outwards, it thrusts it back into the physical substance of the earth. It thrusts it back into the air. And just as one sees with the physical eye physical bats fluttering about, one can also see these corresponding spirit-formations which emanate from the bats fluttering through the air; they sough through the spaces of the air. We know that air consists of oxygen, nitrogen and other constituents, but this is not all; it also consists of the spirit-emanations of bats.

Strange and paradoxical as it may sound, this dream-order of the bats sends little spectres out into the air, which then unite into a general mass. In geology the matter below the earth, which is a rock-mass of a soft consistency like porridge, is called magma. We might also speak of a spirit-magma in the air, which comes from the emanations of bats.

In ancient times when an instinctive clairvoyance prevailed, people were very susceptible to this spirit magma, just as today many people are very susceptible to what is of a material nature, for instance, bad smelling air. This might certainly be regarded as somewhat vulgar, whereas in the ancient instinctive time of clairvoyance people were susceptible to the bat-residue which is present in the air.

They protected themselves against this. And in many Mysteries there were special formulas whereby people could inwardly arm themselves, so that this bat-residue might have no power over them. For as human beings we do not only inhale oxygen and nitrogen with the air, we also inhale these emanations of the bats. Modern people, however, are not interested in letting themselves be protected against these bat-remains, but whereas in certain conditions they are highly sensitive, let us say, to bad smells, they are highly insensitive to the emanations of the bats. It can really be said that they swallow them down without feeling the least trace of repulsion. It is quite extraordinary that people who are otherwise really prudish just swallow down what contains the stuff of which I have spoken. Nevertheless this too enters into the human being. Certainly it does not enter into the physical or etheric body, but it enters into the astral body.

Yes, you see, we here find remarkable connections. Initiation science everywhere leads into the inner aspect of relationships; this bat-residue is the most craved-for nutriment of what I have described in lectures here as the Dragon. But this bat-residue must first be breathed into the human being. The Dragon finds his surest foothold in human nature when man allows his instincts to be imbued with these emanations of the bats. There they seethe. And the dragon feeds on them and grows—in a spiritual sense, of course—gaining power over people, gaining power in the most manifold ways. This is something against which modern man must again protect himself : and the protection should come from what has been described here as the new form of Michael's fight with the Dragon. The increase in inner strength which man gains when he takes up into himself the Michael impulse as it has been described here, this is his safeguard against the nutriment which the Dragon desires; this is his protection against the unjustified bat-emanations in the atmosphere.

If one has the will to penetrate into these inner world-connections, one must not shrink back from facing the truths contained in them. For today the generally accepted form of the search for truth does not in any way lead to actuality, but at most to something even less actual than a dream, to Maya. Reality must of necessity be sought in the domain where all physical existence is regarded as interwoven with spiritual existence. We can only find our way to reality, when this reality is studied and observed, as has been done here in the present lectures.

In everything good and in everything evil, in some way or other beings are present. Everything in world-connections is so ordered that its relation to other beings can be recognized. For the materialistically minded, butterflies flutter, birds fly, bats flit. But this can really be compared to what often happens with a not very artistic person, who adorns the walls of his room with all manner of pictures which do not belong to each other, which have no inner connection. Thus for the ordinary observer of nature, what flies through the world also has no inner connection; because he sees none. But everything in the cosmos has its own place, because just from this very place it has a relation to the cosmos in its totality. Be it butterfly, bird, or bat, everything has its own meaning within the world-order.

As to those who today wish to scoff, let them scoff. People already have other things to their credit in the sphere of ridicule. Celebrated scholars have declared that meteor-stones cannot exist, because iron cannot fall from heaven, and so on. Why then should people not also scoff at the functions of the bats, about which I have spoken today? Such things, however, should not divert us from the task of imbuing our civilization with a knowledge of spiritual truths.

LECTURE VI

28th October, 1923

Before we proceed to the study of the other members of the animal, plant and mineral kingdoms, which are connected with man, we must first cast a glance at the development of man himself, and call to mind various descriptions already familiar to us through books or lectures in a comprehensive survey.

If we go for instruction to present-day science, we are usually told that it is necessary to investigate how the higher, the so-called higher beings and human kingdoms have evolved out of what is lifeless, out of so-called inorganic substances or forces.

A true conception of evolution reveals something essentially different. It reveals—as you will have been able to gather from my "Occult Science"—that man in his present form is the being who has the longest evolution behind him, an evolution which reaches back to the time of ancient Saturn. We must therefore say that man is the oldest creation within the evolution of our earth. It was only during the Sun-period that the animal kingdom was added, then during the Moon-period the plant kingdom; and the mineral kingdom, as we know it today, is in fact only an Earth-product, something which was only added during the Earth-period of evolution.

Let us now consider man in his present form, and ask ourselves: What is the oldest part of man according to his evolutionary history? It is the human head. This human head received its first rudiments at a time when the Earth was in the Saturn-metamorphosis. It is true that the Saturn-condition was composed entirely of warmth-substance, and the human head was then actually flowing, weaving, surging warmth; it then acquired gaseous form during the Sun-period, and fluidic form during the Moon-period, when it became a liquid, flowing entity; and only during the Earth-period did it receive solid form with its bony casing. We must therefore say that a being of which it is difficult to gain a conception through external forms of knowledge existed during the time of ancient Saturn, and of this being the human head is the descendant. And simultaneously with the formation of man's head—this can be gathered from my recent descriptions—simultaneously with this rudimentary origin of the human head during the Saturn-period, the first rudiments of the being of the butterflies also came into existence. Later we shall make a more exact study of the nature of the other insects, but to begin with let us strictly focus our attention on the being of the butterfly. When we follow the course of evolution from the ancient Saturn-period onwards until today, until Earth-existence, we must say : At that time the rudiments of the human head came into existence in a form of very delicate substantiality; and at the same time there arose everything which now flutters through the air as the world of the butterflies. Both these evolutions proceeded further. Man developed his inner being, so that to an ever greater degree he became a being manifesting a soul-nature, which works from within outwards, a being whose development depends upon a radiating from within outwards (a diagram was drawn). The butterfly, on the other hand, is a being upon whose exterior the cosmos may be said to lavish all its beauties. The butterfly is a creature upon which everything of beauty and majesty in the cosmos—as this has been described to you—has, as it were, alighted, together with the dust, on its wings. We must, therefore, picture the being of the butterfly as a mirror which reflects the beauties of the upper cosmos. The human being takes up into himself, encloses within himself, what is of the nature of the upper cosmos, and thus becomes inwardly ensouled. It is like a concentration of the cosmos which then streams outwards, itself giving form to the human head, so that in the human head we have something formed from within outwards. But in the being of the butterfly we have what is formed from outside inwards. For one whose clair-voyant vision can look directly at these things, there is some-thing really tremendous to be learned if he sets to work in the following way. He says : I wish to fathom the mysteries, the most ancient mysteries, the Saturn-mysteries of the human head; I wish to know the true nature of the forces which have held sway inside the skull. He must then let his attention be directed to what is everywhere to be seen outside, to what everywhere streams inwards from outside. *To learn to know the nature of man and the marvel of thine own head, study the marvel of how the butterfly came to be outside in nature.* This is the great lesson imparted by the study of the cosmos through direct spiritual observation.

Evolution then proceeded from the Saturn-period to the Sun-period, and now a being came into existence possessed of a further development, an air-development, an air-meta-morphosis, of the head; but to this there was added in very delicate substance what later became the breast-system, be-came the breathing-and-heart systems of man. In Saturn we have as the essential metamorphosis what produced the human head. When we come to the Sun-period we have the head-breast-man; for it was now that man's breast-system was added. At the same time, however, there already came into existence, in the later part of the Saturn-period and the earlier part of the Sun-period, what must now be seen as having its representative in the eagle. The bird kingdom arose in the first part of the Sun-period, and in the second part of the Sun-period there arose the first rudiments of that kingdom of the animals which are in fact breast-animals, as, for in-stance, the lion—other breast-animals, too, but the lion as their representative. So that the first rudiments of these animals go back to the time of old Sun.

From this you can see what a stupendous difference is present between the evolution of even the higher animals and that of man. In the future I shall still have to speak about the transitional animals, to which belongs the world of the

apes, but today my intention is just to gather things together
into a general concept. You see what an immense difference
exists between the formation of man and the formation of
the higher animals.

In the case of human evolution it was the head which first
took form. All the other organs are, as it were, appended;
they may be said to be appended to the formation of the
head. In cosmic evolution man's development proceeds from
his head downwards. On the other hand the lion, for example,
first came into existence during the old Sun-period, during
the second part of the old Sun-period, as a breast-animal, as
an animal with a powerful breathing-system, but with a head
still very small and poorly developed. And only in later times
when the sun separated from the earth, working from outside, only then did the head develop out of the breast. Thus
the development of the lion was such that it evolved from
the breast upwards, whereas the human being evolved from
the head downwards. This constitutes an immense difference
in evolution as a whole.

And when we now proceed to the Moon-metamorphosis
of the earth, because the Moon represented the water-condition, because the Moon was fluidic—though it certainly developed a horny substance in its later period—it was only
then that the human being needed a further extension downwards. The rudiments of the digestive-system took form. During the old Sun-period, while man possessed only what was
of the nature of air, undulating, scintillating with light, all he
required for the purpose of nourishment was a breathing-
apparatus shut off from below; man was head-and-breathing
organism. Now, during the Moon-period, he acquired a
digestive system, thereby becoming a being of head, breast
and abdomen. And because everything in the old Moon was
still watery substance, during this old Moon-period the human
being had outgrowths which buoyed him up as he swam
through the water. Arms and legs can first be spoken of only
during the Earth-period, when the force of gravity was working, giving form to what is primarily adjusted in accordance

with the directions of gravity, namely the limb-system. This, therefore, belongs only to the Earth-period. During the Moon-period, however, the digestive system was formed, though still quite differently constituted from what it later became; for man's digestive apparatus did not as yet need to assimilate all that serves the free, independent mobility of the limbs. It was still an essentially different digestive system; this was later metamorphosed into the digestive apparatus appropriate to the Earth. It was, however, during the Moon-period that man first acquired his digestive system.

And then it came about further that to the descendants of the butterflies, of the birds and of such species as are represented by the lion, those animals were added which are predominantly adapted to digestion. Thus, during the Moon-period we have the addition of those animals which are represented by the cow.

How then did the development of the cow proceed in contradistinction to that of the human being? Here matters were such that in this old Moon-period it was first and foremost the cow's digestive apparatus that was formed; then, only after the moon had separated, the breast-organs developed out of the digestive system, as did also the peculiarly formed head. Whereas man began his development with the head, adding to this the breast, and finally the digestive organs; whereas the lion began with the breast-organs, adding to these the head, and then, during the old Moon-period, acquiring the digestive organs together with man; in the case of the animals represented by the cow, we have first, as primary origin, the digestive organs, and then, growing out from these as further development, the formation of the organs of breast and head. So you see, man developed from the head downwards, the lion from the breast both upwards and downwards; the cow developed breast and head entirely from the digestive organs, developed, that is to say—if we compare the cow with the human being—entirely in an upwards direction, developed towards heart and head. This is the correct view of human evolution.

Here the question naturally arises : Is it only the cow which was, as it were, the companion thus associated with man's evolution? This is not entirely so, for whenever one or other planetary metamorphosis takes place, the earlier creatures develop further, while at the same time new ones come into existence. The cow already came into being during the first phase of the Moon-metamorphosis. Then, however, other animals were added, which acquired their very earliest rudiments in the last phase of the Moon-metamorphosis. These could not, for example, take part in the departure of the moon, for it was already outside. Nor could they participate in what this departure brought about, namely the drawing forth, as it were, from the cow's belly of the organs of heart and head. These creatures, which made their appearance later, remained stationary at the stage which is determined in man by the digestion, the stage which man carries with him in his abdomen.

And just as the eagle and the butterflies are constituted in relation to the head, the lion in relation to the breast, the cow in relation to the abdomen (though it is the animal which was also able to develop all the upper organs at a later period of evolution), so the amphibians and reptiles, such as toads, frogs, snakes, lizards, are distributed, if I may put it so, among the lower organs of the human being, those of the human digestive system. They are simply digestive organs which came into existence as animals.

BUTTERFLIES	BIRDS, LIONS	COWS, REPTILES, AMPHIBIANS, FISHES
Saturn	*Sun*	*Moon*
Head	Head-Breast	Head-Breast-Abdomen

These last creatures appeared during the second Moon-period in an extremely crude form, and were in fact walking stomachs and entrails, walking stomachs and intestinal tubes. And only later, during the earth-period, did they also acquire a still not particularly distinguished-looking head-system. Only look at the frogs and toads, or the snakes. They came into existence simply and solely as animals of digestion, at a late period, at a time when man could still only append his digestive apparatus to what he had already acquired during an earlier period.

And in the Earth-period, when man acquired his limb-system under the influence of gravity and earth-magnetism, the tortoises—we may take the tortoises as representative animals in this—actually stretched their head out beyond their armoured shell in a manner more like an organ of the limb-system than a head. And now we can understand how it is that in the case of the amphibians and reptiles the head is formed in such an uncouth way. Its form is such that one really has the feeling—and rightly so—that here one passes directly from the mouth into the stomach. There is hardly any intermediary.

When we study man in this way and apportion his being among his animal contemporaries, we must assign what is comprised in the reptiles and amphibians to the human activity of digestion. And one can actually say : Just as man carries around in his intestines the products of his digestion, so does the cosmos carry around—indirectly by way of the earth—the toads, snakes, and frogs in the cosmic intestine which it formed in the watery-earthly element of the Earth. On the other hand, all that is more connected with human propagation, which appeared in its earliest rudiments in the very last phase of the Moon-period, and only developed fully during the Earth-metamorphosis, with this the fishes are allied, the fishes and still lower animals. So that we have to regard the fishes as late arrivals of evolution, as creatures which only joined the company of the other animals at a time when man added his generative organs to those of digestion. The snake is the intermediary between the organs of reproduction and digestion. Rightly viewed in regard to human nature, what does the snake represent? It represents the so-called renal canal; it originated in world-evolution at the same time as the renal canal was developed in man.

Thus we can follow in a correct way how the human

being, beginning with his head, evolved downwards, how the earth drew forth from him the limb-system, providing what this limb-system required in order to establish itself in the earth-equilibrium of gravity and magnetic forces. And simultaneously with this evolution downwards the different classes of the animals took form.

In this way we get a true picture of the evolution of the earth with its creatures. And in accordance with this evolution these creatures have developed in such a way that they present themselves to us as they are today. When you look at the butterflies and the birds you certainly have earthly forms; but you know from previous descriptions that the butterfly is really a light-being and the earthly substance has, as it were, only alighted upon it. If the butterfly itself could tell you what it is, it would announce to you that it has a body formed of light, and that, as I have already said, it carries about what has alighted upon it in the way of earthly matter like luggage, like something external to itself. Similarly one can say that the bird is a creature of warm air, for the true bird is the warm air which is diffused throughout its body; all else is its luggage which it carries with it through the world. These creatures, which even today have still preserved their nature of light and warmth, and are really only clothed with a terrestrial, an earthly, a watery vesture—these beings were the very earliest to arise in the whole of earth-evolution. The very forms, too, possessed by these beings can remind one, who is able to survey the time which man passes through in the spiritual world before his descent into earthly life, of what is experienced in the spiritual world. Certainly they are earthly forms, for earthly matter has alighted upon them. But if we conceive rightly the fluttering, weaving being of light which is the real butterfly, thinking away everything of an earthly nature which has alighted upon it; if we think away from the bird everything of earth which has alighted upon it; if we picture the assembly of forces which makes of the bird a being of warm air, taking account also of the nature of its plumage—in reality just shining rays; if we imagine all this, then these creatures (which only look as they do because of their outer vestment, and of their size appropriate to this outer vestment) remind us of the beings which man knew before his descent to the earth, and of the fact that the human being has made this descent to the earth. Then one who can thus gaze into the spiritual world says to himself : In the butterflies, in the birds, we have something reminiscent of those spirit-forms among which man dwelt before he descended to the earth, of the beings of the higher hierarchies. Looked at with understanding, butterflies and birds are a memory—transformed into miniature and metamorphosed—of those forms which man had around him as spirit-forms before he descended into Earth-evolution. Because earth-substance is heavy and must be overcome, the butterflies contract into miniature the gigantic form which is in reality theirs. If you could separate from a butterfly everything of the nature of earth-substance, it would be able, as spirit-being, as a being of light, to expand to archangelic form. In those creatures which inhabit the air we have the earthly images of what exists in higher regions in a spiritual way. This is why, in the time of instinctive clairvoyance, it was the natural thing in artistic creation to derive from the forms of the winged creatures the symbolic form, the pictorial form, of the beings of the higher hierarchies. This has its inner justification. And looked at fundamentally the physical forms of the butterflies and the birds are really the physical metamorphoses of spiritual beings. It is not the spiritual beings themselves which have undergone metamorphosis, but these forms are their metamorphosed image-picture; naturally, the beings themselves are different.

You will, therefore, also find it comprehensible if, returning to something which I have already discussed, I again draw what follows in a diagram.* I told you that the butterfly, which is essentially a being of light, continually sends spiritualized earth-matter out into the cosmos during its life-time. I should now like to call this spiritualized earth-substance,

* See p. 87.

which is sent forth into the cosmos—borrowing a term customary in solar physics—the butterfly corona. Thus the butterfly corona continually streams forth into the cosmos. But into this butterfly corona there rays what the bird-kingdom yields up to the cosmos every time a bird dies, so that the spiritualized matter from the bird-kingdom is rayed into the corona and out into the cosmos. Thus in spiritual perception one beholds a shimmering corona emanating from the butterfly kingdom—in accordance with certain laws this is maintained in winter also—and in a more ray-like form, introduced into it, one beholds what streams out from the birds.

You see, when the human being has the impulse to descend from the spiritual world to the physical world, it is the butterfly corona, this remarkable outstreaming of spiritualized earth-substance, which first calls him into earthly existence. And the rays of the bird-corona, these are experienced more as forces which draw him. Now you perceive an even higher significance in what has its life in the encircling air. In what lives and weaves in physical reality one must everywhere seek for the spiritual. And it is only when one seeks for the spiritual that one first comes upon the significance of the individual categories of beings. The earth entices man back into incarnation by sending forth into world-space the shining radiance of the butterfly-corona and the rays of the bird-corona. It is these things which once again call man back into a new earthly existence after he has spent a certain period of time between death and re-birth in the purely spiritual world. It is, therefore, not to be wondered at if man finds it difficult to unravel the complicated feelings which he rightly experiences when beholding the world of the butterflies and the birds. For the true reality of these feelings dwells deep in the unconsciousness. What really works in them is the remembrance of a longing for a new earthly existence.

This again is connected with something I have often explained to you, namely that the human being, when he has departed from the earth through the portal of death, actually disperses his head, and that then the remainder of his organism—naturally in regard to its forces, not in regard to its matter—becomes metamorphosed into the head of the next earthly existence. Thus man is striving towards his head when he is striving towards his descent. And it is the head which is the first part of the human embryo to develop in a form which already resembles the later human form. That all this is so is due to the fact that this directing of the formative element towards the head is intimately connected with what works and weaves in the world of the flying creatures, by means of which man is drawn out of supersensible into sensible existence.

When the human being, during the embryonic period, has first acquired his head organization, he then forms out of earthly existence, moulding it within the mother's body, what is connected with the digestive organization, and so on. Just as the upper part, the head-formation, is connected with what is of the nature of warmth and air, with the warmth-light element, so what is now added during the embryonic period is connected with the earthly-fluid element and is a reflection of what man acquired later in evolution. This earthly-fluid element must, however, be prepared in a quite special way, within the mother's body. If it took its form only from what is distributed outside in the tellurian, in the earthly world, it would develop only the lower animal-forms of the amphibians and reptiles, or of the fishes and even lower creatures.

The butterfly rightly regards itself as a being of light, the bird as a being of warm air, but this is impossible for the lower animals—amphibians, reptiles, fishes. Let us first consider the fishes as they are today, as they come into existence subject to external formative forces which work upon them from without, whereas they work from within upon man. A fish lives primarily in the element of water. But water is certainly not just the combination of hydrogen and oxygen which it is for the chemist. Water is permeated by all possible kinds of cosmic forces. Stellar forces enter into water. No fish would be able to live in water if it were merely a homogeneous combination of hydrogen and oxygen. Just as the

butterfly feels itself to be a light-being, and the bird a being
of warm air, so the fish feels itself as an earthly-watery being.
But the fish does not feel the actual water which it sucks in as
its own being. A bird does feel the air which it inhales as its
own being. Thus the bird actually feels what enters into it as
air, and is everywhere diffused through it, as its own being;
this air which is diffused through the bird and warmed by it,
this is its being. The fish has water within it, yet the fish does
not feel itself as the water; the fish feels itself to be what encloses the water, what surrounds the water. It feels itself to be
the glittering sheath or vessel enclosing the water. But the
water itself is felt by the fish as an element foreign to it, which
passes out and in, and, in doing so, brings the air which the
fish needs. Yet air and water are felt by the fish as something foreign. In its physical nature the fish feels the water
as something foreign to it. But the fish has also its etheric and
astral body. And it is just this which is the remarkable thing
about the fish; because it really feels itself to be the vessel,
and the water this vessel encloses remains connected with all
the rest of the watery element, the fish experiences the etheric
as that in which it actually lives. It does not feel the astral as
something belonging to itself.

Thus the fish has the peculiar characteristic that it is so
entirely an etheric creature. It feels itself as the physical vessel
for the water. It feels the water within itself as part and
parcel with all the waters of the world. Moisture is everywhere, and in this moisture the fish at the same time experiences the etheric. For earthly life fishes are certainly dumb,
but if they could speak and could tell you what they feel,
then they would say : "I am a vessel, but the vessel contains
the all-pervading element of water, which is the bearer of the
etheric element. It is in the etheric that I am really swimming." The fish would say : "Water is only Maya; the reality
is the etheric, and it is in this that I really swim." Thus the
fish feels its life as one with the life of the earth. This is the
peculiar thing about the fish : it feels its life as the life of the
earth, and therefore it takes an intimate part in everything

which the earth experiences during the course of the year, experiencing the outgoing of the etheric forces in summer, the drawing-back of the etheric forces in winter. The fish experiences something which breathes in the whole earth. The fish perceives the etheric element as the breathing process of the earth.

Dr. Wachsmuth* once spoke here about the breathing of the earth. This was a very beautiful exposition. If a fish had learned the art of lecturing, it could have given the very same lecture here out of its own experience, for it perceives all that was described in this lecture from having itself followed all the phenomena in question! The fish is the creature which takes part in a quite extraordinary way in the breathing-life of the earth during the cycle of the year, because what is important for the fish is the etheric life-element, which surges out and in, drawing all other breathing-processes with it.

It is otherwise with the reptiles and with the amphibians; with the frogs, for instance, which are remarkably characteristic in this respect. These creatures are less connected with the etheric element of the cosmos; they are connected to a greater degree with its astral element. If one were to ask a fish: "How are things with you?" it would answer: "Well, yes, here on earth I have become an earthly creature, formed out of the earthly-moist elements; but my real life is the life of the whole earth with its cosmic breathing." This is not so with the frog; here matters are essentially different. The frog shares in the general astrality diffused everywhere.

In regard to the plants I told you—and I shall speak further of this—how the astrality of the cosmos above comes into contact with the blossoms. The frog is connected with this astrality, with what may be called the astral body of the earth, just as the fish is connected with the earth's etheric body. The fish possesses its astrality more for itself. The frog possesses its etheric body very strongly for itself, much more strongly than does the fish; but the frog lives in the general astrality; so that it actually shares in those astral processes

* See *The Etheric Formative Forces in Cosmos, Earth and Man* by Günter Wachsmuth.

which play their part in the year's course, where the earth
lets its astrality play into the evaporation of water and its
re-descent. Here the materialistically minded person naturally
says that the evaporation of water is caused by aero-dynamic,
or, if you will, aero-mechanical forces of one kind or another;
these cause the ascent. Drops are formed, and when they
become heavy enough they fall downwards. But this is almost
as though one were to put forward a similar theory about the
circulation of the human blood, without taking into considera-
tion the fact that in the blood-circulation life is everywhere.
In the same way there lives in the circulation of water, with
its upwards and downwards urge, the astral atmosphere of the
earth, the earth's astrality. And I am telling you no fairy-tale
when I say that it is just the frogs—this is also the case with
the other amphibians, but to a less pronounced degree—which
live together with this play of the astrality which manifests in
weather-conditions, in meteorology. It is not only that frogs
are accepted—as you know—in a naïve way as weather-
prophets, but they experience this astral play so wonderfully
because they are placed with their own astrality right into the
astrality of the earth. Certainly the frog does not say "I have
a feeling" but it is the bearer of the feelings which the earth
has in wet spells, in dry spells, and so on. And this is why
in certain weather-conditions you have the more or less beautiful (or ugly) frogs' concert. For this is the frogs' way of
expressing what they experience together with the astral body
of the earth. It is really true that they do not croak unless
they are moved to do so by what comes from the whole
cosmos; they live with the astrality of the earth.

So we can say that the fish, living in the earthly-watery
element naturally participates to a great degree in the life of
the earth: thus we have in the fish earthly life-conditions, in
the frogs, earthly feeling-conditions—as also in the various
species of reptiles and amphibians. Further, if we wish to
study the human digestive organism, we must say that it has
developed from within outwards. But if we wish to study how
it functions, we must turn to the world of amphibians and

reptiles, for to them there comes from outside what permeates the human being as inner forces through his digestive apparatus. It is with the same forces by means of which man digests, that the outer cosmos, outer nature, forms snakes, toads, lizards and frogs. And whoever wishes to make a correct study—excuse me, but there is nothing ugly in nature, everything must be spoken about objectively—whoever wishes to study the inner nature of, let us say, the human large intestine with its power of excretion, must study the toads outwardly; for there comes to the toads from outside what works from within outwards in the human large intestine. Certainly this does not lend itself to such beautiful descriptions as what I had to say about the butterflies; but in nature everything must be taken with objective impartiality.

In this way, you see, you also gain a picture of how the earth, from its side, shares in the life of the cosmos. Turn your attention to what may be called the earth's excretory organs; the earth excretes not only the nearly lifeless products of human excretion, but it excretes what is living, and among its actual excretions are the toads. In them the earth rids itself of what it is unable to use.

From all this you can see how the outer in nature always corresponds with the inner. Whoever says: "No Creative Spirit penetrates the inner being of nature", simply does not know that everywhere in the external world this inner quality is present. We can study the entire human being in regard to his inner nature, if we understand what weaves and lives outside in the cosmos. We can study him, this human being, from head to limb-system, if we study what is present in the outer world. World and man belong together in every respect. And one can even say that this could be represented in a diagram, showing the circumference of a large circle concentrating its force in a point. The large circle forms a smaller circle within, produced by a raying outwards from the point. The smaller circle again forms an even smaller small circle; this is again produced by a raying-outwards of what is within. This circle again forms another such circle. What is comprised in the human being streams still further outwards. Thus the outer of the human being comes into contact with the inner of the cosmos. The point where our senses come in contact with the world is where the part of man which reaches from within outwards comes into contact with what reaches in the cosmos from outside inwards.* In this sense man is a little world, a microcosm over against the macrocosm. But he contains all the wonders and secrets of this macrocosm, only in the reversed direction of development.

It would be something very adverse to the further evolution of the earth if things were only as I have so far described them; then the earth would excrete the beings of the toads, and would one day perish just as physical man must perish, without any continuation. So far, however, we have only considered man's connection with the animals, and have built only a slight bridge over to the being of the plants. We shall now have to penetrate further into the plant-kingdom, and then into the kingdom of mineral-being, and we shall see how the mineral-being arose during the Earth-period—how, for instance, the rock-formations of our primeval mountains were laid down, bit by bit, by the plants, and how, bit by bit, the limestone mountains were laid down by the subsequent animals. The mineral kingdom is the deposit of the plant- and animal-kingdom, and it is actually the deposit of the lowest animals. The toads do not contribute very much to the mineral element of the earth; the fishes, too, comparatively little; but the lower animals and the plants contribute a very great deal. The lower creatures, those plated with flinty and chalky armour, or having merely chalky shells, deposit what they have first formed from their own animal—or their plant— natures, and the mineral then disintegrates. And when this mineral substance disintegrates, a power of the highest order takes hold of just these products of mineral disintegration and from them builds up new worlds. The mineral element in any particular place can become of all things the most important.

When we follow the course of Earth-evolution—warmth-

* In the absence of the author's diagram this passage is obscure.

condition, air-condition, water-condition, mineral-earthly condition—the human head has participated in all these metamorphoses, the mineral metamorphosis being the first to work
outwards in the disintegrating skeleton of the head—though
it still retains a certain vitality. But this human head has
participated in the earthly-mineral metamorphosis in a way
which is even more apparent. In the centre of the human
head within the structure of the brain there is an organ
shaped like a pyramid, the pineal gland. This pineal gland,
situated in the vicinity of the corpus quadrigemina and the
optic thalamus secretes out of itself the so-called brain sand,
minute lemon-yellow stones which lie in little heaps at one
end of the pineal gland, and which are in fact the mineral
element in the human head. If they do not lie there, if man
does not bear this brain-sand, this mineral element, within
him, he becomes an idiot or a cretin. In the case of normal
people the pineal gland is comparatively large. In cretins
pineal glands have been found which are actually no larger
than hemp seeds; these cannot secrete the brain-sand.

It is actually in this mineral deposit that the spirit-man is
situated; and this already indicates that what is living cannot
harbour the spirit, but that the human spirit needs the non-
living as its centre-point, that this is above all things necessary
to it as independent living spirit.

It was a beautiful progression which led us from the but-
terfly-head-formation, the bird-head-formation, downwards to
the reptiles and fishes. We will now re-ascend and study what
will give us as much satisfaction as the kingdom of the animals—the kingdoms of the plants and the minerals. And just
as we have been able to gather teachings about the past from
the animal kingdom, so shall we be able to derive from the
mineral kingdom hope for the future of the earth. At the
same time it will naturally still be necessary in the following
lectures to enter into the nature of transitional animals from
the most varied aspects, for in this survey I have only been
able to touch upon the animals of principal significance,
which, so to say, appear at the key-points of evolution.

Part Three

The Plant-World and the Elemental Nature-Spirits

The World-Word is not some combination of syllables gathered from here or there, but the World-Word is the harmony of what sounds forth from countless beings.

LECTURE VII

2nd November, 1923

To the outwardly perceptible, visible world there belongs the invisible world, and these, taken together, form a whole. The marked degree to which this is the case first appears in its full clarity when we turn our attention away from the animals to the plants.

Plant-life, as it sprouts and springs forth from the earth, immediately arouses our delight, but it also provides access to something which we must feel as full of mystery. In the case of the animal, though certainly its will and whole inner activity have something of the mysterious, we nevertheless recognize that this will is actually there, and is the cause of the animal's form and outer characteristics. But in the case of the plants, which appear on the face of the earth in such magnificent variety of form, which develop in such a mysterious way out of the seed with the help of the earth and the encircling air—in the case of the plant we feel that some other factor must be present in order that this plant-world may arise in the form it does.

When spiritual vision is directed to the plant-world, we are immediately led to a whole host of beings, which were known and recognized in the old times of instinctive clairvoyance, but which were afterwards forgotten and today remain only as names used by the poet, names to which modern man ascribes no reality. To the same degree, however, in which we deny reality to the beings which whirl and weave around the plants, to that degree do we lose the understanding of the plant-world. This understanding of the plant-world, which, for instance, would be so necessary for the art of healing, has been entirely lost to present-day humanity.

We have already recognized a very significant connection between the world of the plants and the world of the butterflies; but this too will only come rightly before our souls when we look yet more deeply into the whole weaving and working of plant-life.

Plants send down their roots into the ground. Anyone who can observe what they really send down and can perceive the roots with spiritual vision (for this he must have) sees how the root-nature is everywhere surrounded, woven around, by elemental nature spirits. And these elemental spirits, with an old clairvoyant perception designated as gnomes and which we may call the root-spirits, can actually be studied by an imaginative and inspirational world-conception, just as human life and animal life can be studied in the sphere of the physical. We can look into the soul-nature of these elemental spirits, into this world of the spirits of the roots.

These root-spirits, are, so to say, a quite special earth-folk, invisible at first to outer view, but in their effects so much the more visible; for no root could develop if it were not for what is mediated between the root and the earth-realm by these remarkable root-spirits, which bring the mineral element of the earth into flux in order to conduct it to the roots of the plants. Naturally I refer to the underlying spiritual process.

These root-spirits, which are everywhere present in the earth, get a quite particular sense of well-being from rocks and from ores (which may be more or less transparent). But they enjoy their greatest sense of well-being, because here they are really at home, when they are conveying what is mineral to the roots of the plants. And they are completely enfilled with an inner element of spirituality which we can only compare with the inner element of spirituality in the human eye, in the human ear. For these root-spirits are in their spirit-nature entirely *sense*. Apart from this they are nothing at all; they consist only of sense. They are entirely sense, and it is a sense which is at the same time *understanding*, which does not only see and hear, but immediately understands what is seen and heard, which in receiving impressions, receives also ideas.

We can even indicate the way in which these root-spirits receive their ideas. We see a plant sprouting out of the earth. The plant comes, as I shall presently show you, into connection with the extra-terrestrial universe; and, particularly at certain seasons of the year, spirit-currents flow from above, from the blossom and the fruit of the plant down into the roots below, streaming into the earth. And just as we turn our eyes towards the light and see, so do the root-spirits turn their faculty of perception towards what seeps downwards from above, through the plant into the earth. What seeps down towards the root-spirits, that is something which the light has sent into the blossoms, which the sun's warmth has sent into the plants, which the air has produced in the leaves, which the distant stars have brought about in the plant's structures. The plant gathers the secrets of the universe, sinks them into the ground, and the gnomes take these secrets into themselves from what seeps down spiritually to them through the plants. And because the gnomes, particularly from autumn on and through the winter, in their wanderings through ore and rock bear with them what has filtered down to them through the plants, they become those beings within the earth which, as they wander, carry the ideas of the whole universe streaming throughout the earth. We look forth into the wide world. The world is built from universal spirit; it is an embodiment of universal ideas, of universal spirit. The gnomes receive through the plants, which to them are the same as rays of light are to us, the ideas of the universe, and within the earth carry them in full consciousness from metal to metal, from rock to rock.

We gaze down into the depths of the earth, not to seek there below for abstract ideas about some kind of mechanical laws of nature, but to behold the roving, wandering gnomes, which are the light-filled preservers of world-understanding within the earth.

Because these gnomes have immediate understanding of

what they see, their knowledge is actually of a similar nature
to that of man. They are the compendium of understanding,
they are entirely understanding. Everything about them is
understanding, an understanding however, which is universal,
and which really looks down upon human understanding as
something incomplete. The gnomes laugh us to scorn on
account of the groping, struggling understanding with which
we manage to grasp one thing or another, whereas they have
no need at all to make use of thought. They have direct perception of what is comprehensible in the world; and they are
particularly ironical when they notice the efforts people have
to make to come to this or that conclusion. Why should they
do this? say the gnomes—why ever should people give themselves so much trouble to think things over? We know everything we look at. People are so stupid—so say the gnomes—
for they must first think things over.

And I must say that the gnomes become ironical to the
point of ill manners if one speaks to them of logic. For why
ever should people need such a superfluous thing—a training
in thinking? The thoughts are already there. The ideas flow
through the plants. Why don't people stick their noses as deep
into the earth as the plant's roots, and let what the sun says
to the plants trickle down into their noses? Then they would
know something! But with logic—so say the gnomes—there
one can only have odd bits and pieces of knowledge.

Thus the gnomes, inside the earth, are actually the bearers
of the ideas of the universe, of the world-all. But for the earth
itself they have no liking at all. They bustle about in the earth
with ideas of the universe, but they actually hate what is
earthly. This is something from which the gnomes would best
like to tear themselves free. Nevertheless they remain with
the earthly—you will soon see why this is—but they hate it,
for the earthly threatens them with a continual danger. The
earth continually holds over them the threat of forcing them
to take on a particular form, the form of those creatures I
described to you in the last lecture, the amphibians, and in
particular of the frogs and the toads. The feeling of the

gnomes within the earth is really this : If we grow too strongly together with the earth, we shall assume the form of frogs or toads. They are continually on the alert to avoid being caught in a too strong connection with the earth, to avoid taking on earthly form. They are always on the defensive against this earthly form, which threatens them as it does because of the element in which they exist. They have their home in the earthly-moist element; there they live under the constant threat of being forced into amphibian forms. From this they continually tear themselves free, by filling themselves entirely with ideas of the extra-terrestrial universe. The gnomes are really that element within the earth which represents the extra-terrestrial, because they must continually reject a growing together with the earthly; otherwise, as single beings, they would take on the forms of the amphibian world. And it is just from what I may call this feeling of hatred, this feeling of antipathy towards the earthly, that the gnomes gain the power of driving the plants up out of the earth. With the fundamental force of their being they unceasingly thrust away the earthly, and it is this thrusting that determines the upward direction of the plant's growth; they push the plants up with them. It accords with the nature of the gnomes in regard to the earthly to allow the plant to have only its roots in the earth, and then to grow upwards out of the earth-sphere; so that it is actually out of the force of their own original nature that the gnomes push the plants out of the earth and make them grow upwards.

Once the plant has grown upwards, once it has left the domain of the gnomes and has passed out of the sphere of the moist-earthly element into the sphere of the moist-airy, the plant develops what comes to outer physical formation in the leaves. But in all that is now active in the leaves other beings are at work, water-spirits, elemental spirits of the watery element, to which an earlier instinctive clairvoyance gave among others the name of undines. Just as we find the roots busied about, woven-about by the gnome-beings in the vicinity of the ground, and observe with pleasure the upward-striving direction which they give, we now see these water-beings, these elemental beings of the water, these undines in their connection with the leaves.

These undine beings differ in their inner nature from the gnomes. They cannot turn like a spiritual sense-organ outwards towards the universe. They can only yield themselves up to the weaving and working of the whole cosmos in the airy-moist element, and therefore they are not beings of such clarity as the gnomes. They dream incessantly, these undines, but their dream is at the same time their own form. They do not hate the earth as intensely as do the gnomes, but they have a sensitivity to what is earthly. They live in the etheric element of water, swimming and swaying through it, and in a very sensitive way they recoil from everything in the nature of a fish; for the fish-form is a threat to them, even if they do assume it from time to time, though only to forsake it immediately in order to take on another metamorphosis. They dream their own existence. And in dreaming their own existence they bind and release, they bind and disperse the substances of the air, which in a mysterious way they introduce into the leaves, as these are pushed upwards by the gnomes. For at this point the plants would wither if it were not for the undines, who approach from all sides, and show themselves, as they weave around the plants in their dream-like existence, to be what we can only call the world-chemists. The undines dream the uniting and dispersing of substances. And this dream, in which the plant has its existence, into which it grows when, developing upwards, it forsakes the ground, this undine-dream is the world-chemist which brings about in the plant-world the mysterious combining and separation of the substances which emanate from the leaf. We can therefore say that the undines are the chemists of plant-life. They dream of chemistry. They possess an exceptionally delicate spirituality which is really in its element just where water and air come into contact with each other. The undines live entirely in the element of moisture, but they develop their actual inner function when they come to the surface of something watery, be it only to the surface of a water-drop or something else of a watery nature. For their whole endeavour lies in preserving themselves from getting the form of a fish, the permanent form of a fish. They wish to remain in a condition of metamorphosis, in a condition of eternal, endlessly changing transformation. But in this state of transformation in which they dream of the stars and of the sun, of light and of warmth, they become the chemists who now, starting from the leaf, carry the plant further in its formation, after it has been pushed upwards by the power of the gnomes. So the plant develops its leaf-growth, and this mystery is now revealed as the dream of the undines into which the plants grow.

To the same degree, however, in which the plant grows into the dream of the undines, does it now come into another domain, into the domain of those spirits which live in the airy-warmth element, just as the gnomes live in the moist-earthly, and the undines in the moist-airy element. Thus it is in the element which is of the nature of air and warmth that those beings live which an earlier clairvoyant art designated as the sylphs. Because air is everywhere imbued with light, these sylphs, which live in the airy-warmth element, press towards the light, relate themselves to it. They are particularly susceptible to the finer but larger movements within the atmosphere.

When in spring or autumn you see a flock of swallows, which produce as they fly vibrations in a body of air, setting an air-current in motion, then this moving air-current—and this holds good for every bird—is for the sylphs something audible. Cosmic music sounds from it to the sylphs. If, let us say, you are travelling somewhere by ship and the seagulls are flying around it, then in what is set in motion by the seagulls' flight there is a spiritual sounding, a spiritual music which accompanies the ship.

Again it is the sylphs which unfold and develop their being within this sounding music, finding their dwelling-place in the moving current of air. It is in this spiritually sounding, moving element of air that they find themselves at home; and at the same time they absorb what the power of light sends into these vibrations of the air. Because of this the sylphs,

which experience their existence more or less in a state of
sleep, feel most in their element, most at home, where birds
are winging through the air. If a sylph is obliged to move and
weave through air devoid of birds, it feels as though it had
lost itself. But at the sight of a bird in the air something quite
special comes over the sylph. I have often had to describe a
certain event in man's life, that event which leads the human
soul to address itself as "I". And I have always drawn attention to a saying of Jean Paul, that, when for the first time a
human being arrives at the conception of his "I", it is as
though he looks into the most deeply veiled Holy of Holies
of his soul. A sylph does not look into any such a veiled Holy
of Holies of its own soul, but when it sees a bird an ego-
feeling comes over it. It is in what the bird sets in motion as
it flies through the air that the sylph feels its ego. And because
this is so, because its ego is kindled in it from outside, the
sylph becomes the bearer of cosmic love through the atmosphere. It is because the sylph embodies something like a
human wish, but does not have its ego within itself but in
the bird-kingdom, that it is at the same time the bearer of
wishes of love through the universe.

Thus we behold the deepest sympathy between the sylphs
and the bird-world. Whereas the gnome hates the amphibian-
world, whereas the undine is unpleasantly sensitive to fishes,
is unwilling to approach them, tries to avoid them, feels a kind
of horror for them, the sylph, on the other hand, is attracted
towards birds, and has a sense of well-being when it can waft
towards their plumage the swaying, love-filled waves of the
air. And were you to ask a bird from whom it learns to sing,
you would hear that its inspirer is the sylph. Sylphs feel a
sense of pleasure in the bird's form. They are, however, pre-
vented by the cosmic ordering from becoming birds, for they
have another task. Their task is lovingly to convey light to
the plant. And just as the undine is the chemist for the plant,
so is the sylph the light-bearer. The sylph imbues the plant
with light; it bears light into the plant.

Through the fact that the sylphs bear light into the plant,

something quite remarkable is brought about in it. You see, the sylph is continually carrying light into the plant. The light, that is to say the power of the sylphs in the plant, works upon the chemical forces which were induced into the plant by the undines. Here occurs the interworking of sylph-light and undine-chemistry. This is a remarkable plastic activity. With the help of the upstreaming substances which are worked upon by the undines, the sylphs weave out of the light an ideal plant-form. They actually weave the Archetypal Plant within the plant from light, and from the chemical working of the undines. And when towards autumn the plant withers and everything of physical substance disintegrates, then these plant-forms begin to seep downwards, and now the gnomes perceive them, perceive what the world—the sun through the sylphs, the air through the undines—has brought to pass in the plant. This the gnomes perceive, so that throughout the entire winter they are engaged in perceiving below what has seeped into the ground through the plants. Down there they grasp world-ideas in the plant-forms which have been plastically developed with the help of the sylphs, and which now in their spiritual ideal form enter into the ground.

Naturally those people who regard the plant as something purely material know nothing of this spiritual ideal form. Thus at this point something appears which in the materialistic observation of the plant gives rise to what is nothing other than a colossal error, a terrible error. I will sketch this error for you.

Everywhere you will find that materialistic science describes matters as follows : The plant takes root in the ground, above the ground it develops its leaves, finally unfolding its blossoms, within the blossoms the stamens, then the seed-bud. Now—usually from another plant—the pollen from the anthers, from the pollen vessels, is carried over to the germ which is then fructified, and through this the seed of the new plant is produced. The germ is regarded as the female element and what comes from the stamens as the male—indeed matters cannot be regarded otherwise as long as people remain fixed in materialism, for then this process really does look like a fructification. This, however, it is not. In order to gain insight into the process of fructification, that is to say the process of reproduction, in the plant-world, we must be conscious that in the first place it is from what the great chemists, the undines, bring about in the plants, and from what the sylphs bring about, that the plant-form arises, the ideal plant-form which sinks into the ground and is preserved by the gnomes. It is there below, this plant-form. And there within the earth it is now guarded by the gnomes after they have seen it, after they have looked upon it. The earth becomes the mother-womb for what thus seeps downwards. This is something quite different from what is described by materialistic science.

After it has passed through the sphere of the sylphs, the plant comes into the sphere of the elemental fire-spirits. These fire-spirits are the inhabitants of the warmth-light element. When the warmth of the earth is at its height, or is otherwise suitable, they gather the warmth together. Just as the sylphs gather up the light, so do the fire-spirits gather up the warmth and carry it into the blossoms of the plants.

Undines carry the action of the chemical ether into the plants, sylphs the action of the light-ether into the plant's blossoms. And the pollen now provides what may be called little air-ships, to enable the fire-spirits to carry the warmth into the seed. Everywhere warmth is collected with the help of the stamens, and is carried by means of the pollen from the anthers to the seeds and the seed vessels. And what is formed here in the seed-bud is entirely the male element which comes from the cosmos. It is not a case of the seed-vessel being female and the anthers of the stamens being male. In no way does fructification occur in the blossom, but only the preforming of the male seed. The fructifying force is what the fire-spirits in the blossom take from the warmth of the world-all as the cosmic male seed, which is united with the female element. This element, drawn from the forming of the plant has, as I told you, already earlier seeped down into the ground as ideal form, and is resting there below. *For plants the earth is the mother, the heavens the father*. And all that

Male

Fire Spirits

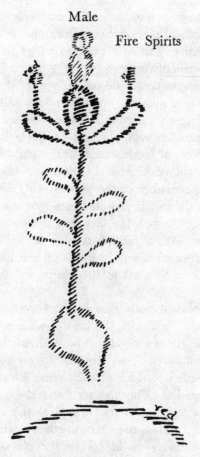

takes place outside the domain of the earth is not the mother-womb for the plant. It is a colossal error to believe that the mother-principle of the plant is in the seed-bud. The fact is that this is the male-principle, which is drawn forth from the universe with the aid of the fire-spirits. The mother comes from the cambium, which spreads from the bark to the wood, and is carried down from above as ideal form. And what now results from the combined working of gnome-activity and fire-spirit activity—this is fructification. The gnomes are, in fact, the spiritual midwives of plant-reproduction. Fructi-fication takes place below in the earth during the winter, when the seed comes into the earth and meets with the forms which the gnomes have received from the activities of the sylphs and undines and now carry to where these forms can meet with the fructifying seeds.

You see, because people do not recognize what is spiritual, do not know how gnomes, undines, sylphs and fire-spirits—which were formerly called salamanders—weave and live together with plant-growth, there is complete lack of clarity about the process of fructification in the plant world. There, outside the earth nothing of fructification takes place, but the earth is the mother of the plant-world, the heavens the father. This is the case in a quite literal sense. Plant-fructification takes place through the fact that the gnomes take from the fire-spirits what the fire-spirits have carried into the seed-bud as concentrated cosmic warmth on the little airships of the anther-pollen. Thus the fire-spirits are the bearers of warmth.

And now you will easily gain insight into the whole process of plant-growth. First, with the help of what comes from the fire-spirits, the gnomes down below instil life into the plant and push it upwards. They are the fosterers of life. They carry the life-ether to the root—the same life-ether in which they themselves live. The undines foster the chemical ether, the sylphs the light-ether, the fire-spirits the warmth ether. And then the fruit of the warmth-ether again unites with what is present below as life. Thus the plants can only be understood when they are considered in connection with all that is circling, weaving and living around them. And one only reaches the right interpretation of the most important process in the plant when one penetrates into these things in a spiritual way.

When once this has been understood, it is interesting to look again at that memorandum of Goethe's where, referring to another botanist, he is so terribly annoyed because people speak of the eternal marriage in the case of the plants above the earth. Goethe is affronted by the idea that marriages should be taking place over every meadow. This seemed to him something unnatural. In this Goethe had an instinctive but very true feeling. He could not as yet know the real facts of the matter, nevertheless he instinctively felt that fructification should not take place above in the blossom. Only he did not as yet know what goes on down below under the ground, he did not know that the earth is the mother-womb of the plants. But, that the process which takes place above in the blossom is not what all botanists hold it to be, this is something which Goethe instinctively felt.

You are now aware of the inner connection between plant and earth. But there is something else which you must take into account.

You see, when up above the fire-spirits are circling around the plant and transmitting the anther-pollen, then they have only *one* feeling, which they have in an enhanced degree, compared to the feeling of the sylphs. The sylphs experience their self, their ego, when they see the birds flying about. The fire-spirits have this experience, but to an intensified degree, in regard to the butterfly-world, and indeed the insect-world as a whole. And it is these fire-spirits which take the utmost delight in following in the tracks of the insects' flight so that they may bring about the distribution of warmth for the seed-buds. In order to carry the concentrated warmth, which must descend into the earth so that it may be united with the ideal form, in order to do this the fire-spirits feel themselves inwardly related to the butterfly-world, and to the insect-creation in general. Everywhere they follow in the tracks of the insects as they buzz from blossom to blossom. And so one really has the feeling, when following the flight of insects, that each of these insects as it buzzes from blossom to blossom, has a quite special aura which cannot be entirely explained from the insect itself. Particularly the luminous, wonderfully radiant, shimmering, aura of bees, as they buzz from blossom to blossom, is unusually difficult to explain. And why? It is because the bee is everywhere accompanied by a fire-spirit which feels so closely related to it that, for spiritual vision, the bee is surrounded by an aura which is actually a fire-spirit. When a bee flies through the air from plant to plant, from tree to tree, it flies with an aura which is actually given to it by a fire-spirit. The fire-spirit does not only gain a feeling of its ego in the presence of the insect, but it wishes to be completely united with the insect.

Through this, however, insects also obtain that power about which I have spoken to you, and which shows itself in a shimmering forth of light into the cosmos. They obtain the power completely to spiritualize the physical matter which unites itself with them, and to allow the spiritualized physical substance to ray out into cosmic space. But just as with a flame it is the warmth in the first place which causes the light to shine, so, above the surface of the earth, when the insects shimmer forth into cosmic space what attracts the human being to descend again into physical incarnation, it is the fire spirits which inspire the insects to this activity, the fire-spirits which are circling and weaving around them. But if the fire-spirits are active in promoting the outstreaming of spiritualized matter into the cosmos, they are no less actively engaged in seeing to it that the concentrated fiery element, the concentrated warmth, goes into the interior of the earth, so that, with the help of the gnomes, the spirit-form, which sylphs and undines cause to seep down into the earth, may be awakened.

This, you see, is the spiritual process of plant-growth. And it is because the subconscious in man divines something of a special nature in the blossoming, sprouting plant that he experiences the being of the plant as full of mystery. The wonder is not spoiled, the magic is not brushed from the dust on the butterfly's wing. Rather is the instinctive delight in the plant raised to a higher level when not only the physical plant is seen, but also that wonderful working of the gnome-world below, with its immediate understanding and formative intelligence, the gnome-world which first pushes the plant upwards. Thus, just as human understanding is not subjected to gravity, just as the head is carried without our feeling its weight, so the gnomes with their light-imbued intellectuality overcome what is of the earth and push the plant upwards. Down below they prepare the life. But the life would die away were it not formed by chemical activity. This is brought to it by the undines. And this again must be imbued with light. And so we picture, from below upwards, in bluish, blackish shades the force of gravity, to which the impulse upwards is given by the gnomes; and weaving around the plant—indicated by the leaves—the undine-force blending and dispersing substances as the plant grows upwards. From above downwards, from the sylphs, light falls into the plants and shapes an idealized plastic form which descends, and is taken up by the mother-womb of the earth; moreover this form is circled around by the fire-spirits which concentrate the cosmic warmth into the tiny seed-points. This warmth is also sent downwards to the gnomes, so that from out of fire and life, they can cause the plants to arise.

And further we now see that essentially the earth is indebted for its power of resistance and its density to the antipathy of the gnomes and undines towards amphibians and fishes. If the earth is dense, this density is due to the antipathy by means of which the gnomes and undines maintain their form. When light and warmth sink down on to the earth, this is first due to that power of sympathy, that sustaining power of sylph-love, which is carried through the air, and then to the sustaining sacrificial power of the fire-spirits, which causes them to incline downwards to what is below themselves. So we may say that, over the face of the earth, earth-density, earth-magnetism and earth-gravity, in their upward-striving aspect, unite with the downward-striving power of love and sacrifice. And in this interworking of the downwards streaming force of love and sacrifice and the upwards streaming force of density, gravity and magnetism, in this interworking, where the two streams meet, plant-life develops over the earth's surface. Plant-life is an outer expression of the interworking of world-love and world-sacrifice with world-gravity and world-magnetism.

From this you have seen with what we have to do when

we direct our gaze to the plant-world, which so enchants, up-
lifts and inspires us. Here real insight can only be gained when
our vision embraces the spiritual, the supersensible, as well
as what is accessible to the physical senses. This enables us
to correct the capital error of materialistic botany, that fructification occurs above the earth. What occurs there is not the
process of fructification, but the preparation of the male
heavenly seed for what is being made ready as the future plant
in the mother-womb of the earth.

LECTURE VIII

3rd November, 1923

Yesterday I spoke to you about the other side of nature-existence, about those supersensible and invisible beings which accompany the beings and processes visible to the senses. An earlier, instinctive vision beheld these beings of the super-sensible world as clearly as we behold the world of the senses. Today, these beings have withdrawn from human view. It is only because this company of gnomes, undines, sylphs and fire-beings is not perceptible in the same way as animals, plants and so on, only to this is it due that man, in the present epoch of his earth-evolution, is not in a position to unfold his soul-spiritual being without the help of his physical and etheric bodies. In the present situation of earth evolution man is obliged to depend upon the etheric body when making use of his soul, and upon the physical body when making use of his spirit. The physical body, which provides the instrument for the spirit, the sense-apparatus, is not adapted to entering into connection with the beings which exist behind the physical world. It is the same with the etheric body, which man must use to develop his soul-being. Through this, if I may put it so, half of his earthly environment escapes him. He passes over everything connected with these elemental beings about which I spoke yesterday. To this world the etheric and physical bodies have no access. We gain an idea of what actually escapes the man of today when we realize what such gnomes, undines, and so on, actually are.

We have, you see, a whole host of lower creatures—lower at the present time—those beings which consist only of a soft mass, which live in the fluid element, and have nothing in the way of an articulated skeleton to give them inner support.

They are creatures which belong to the latest phase of earth-development; creatures which only now, when the earth has already evolved, develop what man—the oldest earth-being—already developed in his head-structure during the time of ancient Saturn. These creatures have not progressed so far as to form within themselves that hardening of the substance which can become the supporting skeleton.

It is the gnomes which, in a spiritual way, make good in the world what the lower orders of the animals up to the amphibians lack. This applies also to the fishes, which have only indications of the skeleton. These lower animal orders only become complete, as it were, through the fact that gnomes exist.

And just because the conditions of the beings in the world are very different, something arises between these lower creatures and the gnomes which I yesterday called antipathy. The gnomes do not wish to become like these lower creatures. They are continually on the watch to protect themselves from assuming their form. As I described to you, the gnomes are extraordinarily clever, intelligent beings. With them intelligence is already implicit in perception; they are in every respect the antithesis of the lower animal world. And whereas they have the significance for plant-growth which I described yesterday, in the case of the lower animal world they actually provide its completion. They supply what this lower animal world does not possess. This lower animal world has a dull consciousness; the gnomes have a consciousness of the utmost clarity. The lower creatures have no bony skeleton, no bony support; the gnomes bind together what works as the force of gravity and make their bodies from this volatile, invisible force, bodies which are, moreover, in constant danger of disintegrating, of losing their substance. The gnomes must ever and again create themselves anew out of gravity, because they continually stand in danger of losing their substance. Because of this, in order to retain their own existence, the gnomes are constantly attentive to what is going on around them. As far as earth-observation goes no being is more attentive than a gnome. It takes note of everything, for it must know everything, grasp everything, in order to preserve its life. A gnome must always be wide awake; if it were to become sleepy, as men often do, this sleepiness would immediately cause its death.

There is a German saying of very early origin which aptly expresses this characteristic of the gnomes, in having always to remain attentive. People say: Pay heed like a goblin. And goblins are in fact the gnomes. So, if one wishes to make some-one attentive, one says to him: Pay heed like a gnome. A gnome is really an attentive being. If one could place a gnome as an object lesson on a front desk in every school classroom, where all could see it, it would be a splendid example for the children to imitate.

The gnomes have yet another characteristic. They are filled with an absolutely unconquerable lust for independence. They trouble themselves little about one another and give their attention only to the world of their own surroundings. One gnome takes little interest in another. But everything else in this world around them, in which they live, this interests them exceedingly.

Now I told you that the human body forms a hindrance to our perceiving such folk as these. The moment this hindrance is removed, these beings are there, just as are the other beings of nature for ordinary vision. Anyone who comes so far as to experience in full consciousness his dreams on falling asleep is well acquainted with these gnomes. You need only recall what I recently published in the "Goetheanum" on the sub-ject of dreams. I said that a dream in no way appears to ordinary consciousness in its true form, but wears a mask. Such a mask is worn by the dream when we fall asleep. We do not immediately escape from the experience of our ordin-ary day consciousness. Reminiscences well up, memory-pictures from life; we perceive symbols, sense-pictures of the inner organs—the heart as a stove, the lungs as wings—all in symbolic form. These are masks. If someone were to see a dream unmasked, if he were actually to pass into the world of sleep without the beings existing there being masked, then, at the moment of falling asleep, he would behold a whole host of goblins coming towards him.

In ordinary consciousness man is protected from seeing these things unprepared, for they would terrify him. The form in which they would appear would actually be copy images of all those qualities in the man which work as forces of destruction. He would perceive all the destructive forces within him, all that continually destroys. These gnomes, if perceived unprepared, would be nothing but symbols of death. Man would be terribly alarmed by them, if in ordinary consciousness he knew nothing about them, and was now confronted by them on falling asleep. He would feel entombed by them—for this is how it would appear—entombed by them over yonder in the astral world. For it is a kind of entombment by the gnomes which, seen from the other side, takes place on falling asleep.

This holds good only for the moment of falling asleep. A further complement to the physical sense-world is supplied by the undines, the water-beings, which continually transform themselves, and which live in connection with the water just as the gnomes live in connection with the earth. These undines—we have learned to know the role they play in plant-growth—also exist as complementary beings to those animals which stand at a somewhat higher stage, which have assumed a more differentiated earthly body. These animals, which have developed into the more evolved fishes, or also into the more evolved amphibians, require scales, require some sort of hard external shell. The forces needed to provide certain creatures with this outer support, this outer skeleton—for these forces the world is indebted to the activity of the undines. The gnomes support spiritually those creatures which are at a quite low stage. Those creatures which must be supported externally, which must be clad in a kind of armour, they owe their protective sheath to the activity of the undines. Thus it is the undines which impart to these somewhat higher animals in a primitive way what we have in the covering of our skull. They make them, as it were, into heads. All these beings which are invisibly present behind the visible world have their great task in the economy of existence. You will always notice that, where materialistic science wishes to explain something of the kind I have just developed, there it breaks down. It is not in a position, for instance, to explain how the lower creatures manage to propel themselves forward in an element which is scarcely harder than they are themselves, because it does not know about the presence of this spiritual support from the gnomes which I have just described. Equally, the formation of an armour-like sheath will always create a difficulty for purely materialistic science, because it does not know that the undines, in their sensitivity to, their avoidance of their own tendency to become lower animals, thrust off from themselves what then appears upon the somewhat higher animals as scales or some other armour-like covering.

Again, in the case of these beings, it is only the body which hinders the ordinary consciousness of today from seeing them just as, for example, it sees the leaves of plants, or the higher animals.

When, however, man falls into a state of deep, dreamless sleep, and yet his sleep is not dreamless, because through the gift of inspiration it has become transparent, then his spiritual gaze perceives the undines rising up out of that astral sea in which, on falling asleep, he was engulfed, submerged by the gnomes. In deep sleep the undines become visible. Sleep extinguishes ordinary consciousness, but the sleep which is illumined by clear consciousness has as its content the wonderful world of ever-changing fluidity, a fluidity which lends itself in every possible way to the metamorphoses of the undines. Just as for day consciousness we have around us beings with firm contours, a clear night consciousness would present to us these ever-changing beings, which themselves well upwards and sink down again like the waves of the sea. All deep sleep in the environment of man is filled with a moving sea of living beings, a moving sea of undines.

Matters are otherwise with the sylphs. They, too, provide a completing element to the being of certain animals, but now in the other direction. The gnomes and undines add what is of the nature of the head to those animals where this is lacking. Birds, however, as I described to you, are actually pure head; they are entirely head-organization. The sylphs add to the birds in a spiritual way what they lack as the bodily complement of their head-organization. They complement the bird-kingdom in regard to what corresponds to the metabolic limb-system in man. If the birds fly about in the air with under-developed legs, so much the more powerfully developed is the limb-system of the sylphs. They may be said to represent in the air, in a spiritual way, what the cow represents below in physical matter. This is why I could say yesterday that it is in connection with the birds that the sylphs have their ego, have what connects them with the earth. Man acquires his ego on the earth. What connects the sylphs with the earth, that is the bird-kingdom. The sylphs are indebted to the bird-kingdom for their ego, or at least for the consciousness of their ego.

Now when someone has slept through the night, has had around him the astral sea, consisting as it does of the most manifold undine-forms, and then wakes up with an awakening dream, then again, if this dream on awakening were not masked in reminiscences of life or sense-pictures of the organs, if he were to see the unmasked dream, he would be confronted by the world of the sylphs. But these sylphs would assume for him a remarkable form; they would appear much as the sun might if it wished to send to men something which would affect them adversely, something which would lull them spiritually to sleep. We shall hear shortly why this is the case. Nevertheless, if someone were to perceive his dream on awakening unmasked, he would see in it an inflowing, an actual inflowing of light. He would also experience this as unpleasant, because the limb-system of these sylphs would, as it were, spin and weave around him. He would feel as though the light were attacking him from all sides, as if the light were

something overwhelming, something to which he was extraordinarily sensitive. Here and there, perhaps, he might also
feel this as a caress of the light. But in all these things I only
wish to indicate to you how the light, with its upholding,
gently touching quality, actually appears in the sylph-form.

And when we come to the fire-beings, we find that they
provide the completing element to the fleeting nature of
the butterflies. A butterfly itself develops as little as possible
of its actual physical body; it lets this be as tenuous as possible. It is, on the contrary, a creature of light. The fire-
spirits appear as beings which complement the butterfly's
body, so that we can get the following impression. If, on the
one hand, we had a physical butterfly before us, and pictured
it greatly enlarged, and on the other side a fire-being—they
are, it is true, rarely together, except in the circumstances
which I mentioned to you yesterday—then, if these two were
welded together, we would get something resembling a winged
man, actually a winged man. We need only increase the size
of the butterfly, and adapt the size of the fire-spirit to human
proportions, and from this we would get something like a
winged man.

This shows you again how the fire-spirits are in fact the
complement to those creatures which are nearest to what is
spiritual; they complement them, so to say, in a downward
direction. Gnomes and undines complement in an upward
direction, towards the head; sylphs and fire-beings complement the birds and butterflies in a downwards direction. Thus
the fire-beings must be brought together with the butterflies.

Now in the same way that man can, as it were, penetrate
through the sleeping-dream, so can he also penetrate through
waking-day life. But here he makes use of his physical body
in quite a robust way. This, too, I have described in articles
in the "Goetheanum". Here also man is totally unable to
perceive how, in his waking life, he could continually see the
fire-beings, in that the fire-beings are inwardly related to his
thoughts, to everything which proceeds from the head-organization. But when a man has progressed so far that he can

remain completely in waking consciousness, but nevertheless stand in a certain sense outside himself, viewing himself from outside as a thinking being, while standing firmly on the earth, then he will become aware how the fire-beings form that element in the world which, when we perceive it, makes our thoughts perceptible from the other side.

Thus the perceiving of the fire-beings can enable man to *see* himself as thinker, not merely to *be* the thinker and, as such, call up the thoughts, but actually to behold how the thoughts run their course. Only then do the thoughts cease to be bound to the human being; then they reveal themselves as *world-thoughts*; they work and weave as impulses in the world. Then one notices that the human head only calls forth the illusion that thoughts are enclosed inside the skull. There they are only reflected; their mirrored images are there. What underlies these thoughts belongs to the sphere of the fire-beings, one sees in these thoughts not only the thoughts themselves, but the thought-content of the world, which, at the same time, is actually an imaginative content. This is the force which enables us to arrive at the realization that thoughts are world-thoughts.

I venture to add : When we behold what is to be seen upon the earth, not from the human bodily nature, but from the sphere of the fire-beings—that is, from the Saturn-nature which has been carried into the Earth—then we gain exactly the picture of the evolution of the earth which I have described in "Occult Science—an Outline". This book is actually so composed that the thoughts appear as the thought-content of the world, seen from the perspective of the fire-beings.

You see, these things have in themselves a deep and real significance. But they also have a deep and real significance for man. Take the gnomes and undines : they are, so to say, in the world which borders on human consciousness; they are already beyond the threshold. Ordinary consciousness is protected from seeing these beings, for the fact is that these beings are not all benevolent. The benevolent beings are, for instance, those which I described yesterday as working in the most varied ways upon plant-growth. But these beings are not all well-disposed. And in the moment when man breaks through into the world wherein they live and are active, he finds there not only the well-disposed beings but the malevolent ones as well. And so one must first form a conception as to which of them are well-disposed and which of them malevolent. This is not so easy, as you will see from the way I must describe the malevolent ones. The main difference between the ill-disposed beings and the well-disposed is that the latter are always drawn more to the plant and mineral kingdoms, whereas the ill-disposed are drawn to the animal and human kingdoms. Some, which are even more malevolent, also desire to approach the kingdoms of the plants and the minerals. But one can gain quite a fair idea of the malevolence which the beings of this realm can have, when one turns to those which are drawn to human beings and animals, wishing in particular to consummate in man what is allotted by the higher hierarchies to the well-disposed beings for the plant and mineral world.

You see, there exist ill-disposed beings from the realm of the gnomes and undines, which make for human beings and animals and bring it about that what they should really impart only to the lower animals appears physically in human beings. Certainly, these things are already present in man, but their aim is that this element should be manifested physically in human beings as well as in animals. Through the presence of these malevolent gnome- and undine-beings, animal and plant life of a low order—parasites—exist in human beings as well as in animals. These malevolent beings are the begetters of parasites. The moment man crosses the threshold of the spiritual world, he at once meets the subtleties of this world. Snares are everywhere, and he must first learn something from the goblins—namely, to be attentive. The spiritualists can never manage this! Everywhere there are snares. Now someone might say : Why then are these malevolent gnome- and undine-beings there, if they engender parasites? Well, if they were not there, man would never be able to develop within himself the force to evolve the structure of his brain. And here we meet something of extraordinary significance.

I will sketch this for you in a diagram. If you think of the human being as consisting of the metabolic-limb-man, of the breast-man, that is, the rhythmic system, and then of the head-man, that is the system of nerves and senses, there are certain things about which you must be quite clear. Here below processes are taking place—let us leave out the rhythmic man—and here above processes are again taking place. If you look at the processes taking place below as a whole, you find that in ordinary life their essential function is usually disregarded. These processes are those of excretion—through the intestines, through the kidneys, and so on—all of them having their outlet in a downwards direction. They are mostly regarded simply as excretory processes. But this is a misinterpretation. Excretion does not take place merely for the purpose of elimination, but to the same degree in which the products of excretion appear, something appears spiritually in the lower man which resembles what the brain is physically above. What occurs in the lower man is a process which is arrested halfway in regard to its physical development. Excretion takes place because the process passes over into the spiritual. In the upper man the process is completed. What below is only spiritual, there assumes physical form. Above we have the physical brain, below a spiritual brain. And if what is eliminated below were to be subjected to a further process, if the changes in its condition were to be continued, then its final metamorphosis would be preliminary to the human brain.

The human brain-mass is the further evolved product of excretion. This is something which is of immense importance, in regard to medicine for instance, and it is something of which doctors in the sixteenth and seventeenth centuries were still fully aware. Of course today people speak in a very derogatory manner—and rightly in many respects—of the old "quack-apothecaries". But this is because they do not know that their potions still contained "mummies" of the spirit.

Naturally this is not intended as a glorification of what has figured as "quackery" in the past centuries, but I am drawing attention to many truths which have connections as deep as those which I have just cited.

It is a fact that the brain is a higher metamorphosis of the products of excretion. Hence the connection between brain-illnesses and intestinal illnesses, and their cure.

You see, because gnomes and undines exist, because there is a real world in which they live, the forces are present, which, proceeding from the lower man, do indeed give rise to parasites, but yet, at the same time, bring about in the upper man the metamorphosis of the products of excretion into the brain. It would be absolutely impossible for us to have a brain, if the world were not so ordered that gnomes and undines can exist.

What holds good for gnomes and undines in regard to the destructive forces—for destruction, disintegration, also proceed in their turn from the brain—this holds good for sylphs and fire-beings, in regard to the constructive forces. Here again the well-disposed sylphs and fire-beings hold themselves aloof from men and animals, and busy themselves with plant-growth in the way I have described; but there are also those which are malevolent. These ill-disposed beings are above all concerned in carrying what should only have its place up above in the regions of air and warmth down into the watery and earthy regions.

Now if you wish to study what happens when these sylph-beings carry what belongs up above down into the watery and earthy regions, look at the belladonna. The belladonna is the plant, which, if I may put it so, has been kissed in its blossoms by the sylphs, and in it what could be beneficent juices have been changed into juices which are poisonous.

Here you have what may be called a displacement of spheres. It is right when the sylphs develop their enveloping forces up above, as I have already described, where the light touches the surface in a formative way—for the bird-world needs this. But if the sylph descends, and makes use below of what it should employ up above in the plant-world, a potent vegetable poison is engendered. Parasitic beings arise through gnomes and undines; through sylphs the poisons which are in fact a heavenly element which has streamed down too deeply on to the earth. When men or certain animals eat the belladonna, which looks like a cherry, except that it conceals itself in the calyx (in the very way it is pressed down you can see what I have just described)—when men or certain animals eat the belladonna, it is fatal to them. But just look at the thrushes and blackbirds; they perch on the belladonna and get from it the best food in the world. It is to their region that what is present in the belladonna belongs.

It is a remarkable thing that animals and man, who in their lower organs are in fact earth-bound, should experience as poison what has become corrupted on the earth in the belladonna, whereas birds such as thrushes and blackbirds, which should really get this in a spiritual way from the sylphs —and indeed through the benevolent sylphs do so obtain it— should be able to assimilate it, even when what belongs up above in their region has been carried downwards to the earth. They find nourishment in what is poison for beings more bound to the earth.

Thus you get a conception of how, on the one side, through gnomes and undines what is of a parasitic nature strives upwards from the earth towards other beings, and of how the poisons filter downwards from above.

When, on the other hand, the fire-beings imbue themselves with those impulses which belong in the region of the butterflies, and are of great use to them in their development—when the fire-beings carry those impulses down into the fruits, there arises—within the species of the almonds, for instance—what appears as the poisonous almonds. This poison is carried into the fruit of the almond trees through the activity of the firebeings. And yet the fruit of the almond could not come into existence at all if beings from this same world of the firebeings did not in a beneficial way burn up, as it were, what is the edible part in other fruits. Only look at the almond. With other fruits you have the white core in the centre and around it the flesh of the fruit. With the almond you have the kernel there in the centre, and around it the flesh of the fruit is quite burnt up. That is the action of the fire-beings. And if this activity miscarries, if what the fire-beings are bringing about is not confined to the brown burnt-up shell, where it can still be beneficial, but something of what should be engaged in developing the almond-shell penetrates into the white kernel, then the almond becomes poisonous.

And so you have gained a picture of those beings which are just on the boundary of the world lying immediately beyond the threshold, and of how, if they carry their impulses to their final issue, they become the bearers of parasites, of poisons, and therewith of illnesses. Now it becomes clear how far man in health raises himself above the forces that take hold of him in illness. For illness springs from the malevolence of these beings who are necessary for the upbuilding of the whole structure of nature, but also for its fading and decay.

These are the things which, arising from instinctive clairvoyance, underlie such intuitions as those of the Indian Brahma, Vishnu and Shiva. Brahma represented the active Being in world-spheres which may legitimately approach man. Vishnu represented those world-spheres which may only approach man in so far as what has been built up must again be broken down, in so far as it must be continually transformed. Shiva represented everything connected with the forces of destruction. And in the earlier stages of the flower of Indian civilization it was said that Brahma is intimately related to all that is of the nature of the fire-beings, and the sylphs; Vishnu with all that is of the nature of sylphs and undines; Shiva with all that is of the nature of undines and gnomes. Generally speaking, when we go back to these more ancient conceptions, we find everywhere the pictorial expressions for what must be sought today as lying behind the secrets of nature.

Yesterday we studied the connection of this invisible folk

with the plant-world; today we have added their connection with the world of the animals. Everywhere beings on this side of the threshold are interlocked with those from beyond it; and beings from beyond the threshold with those on this side. Only when one knows the living interworking of both these kinds of beings does one really understand how the visible world unfolds. Knowledge of the supersensible world is indeed very, very necessary for man, because in the moment when he passes through the gate of death he no longer has the sense-world around him, but now the other world begins to be *his* world. At his present stage of evolution man cannot find right access into the other world unless he has recognized in physical manifestations the written characters which direct him over into this other world; if he has not learned to read in the creatures of the earth, in the creatures of the water, in the creatures of the air, and, indeed, in the creatures of the light, the butterflies, what leads him to the elemental beings which are our companions between death and a new birth. What we see of these beings here between birth and death is, so to speak, their crude, dense part. We only learn to recognize what belongs to them as their supersensible nature when, with insight and understanding, we transfer ourselves into this supersensible world.

LECTURE IX

4th November, 1923

We only learn to know the beings of the sense-world when we observe them in the way they live and act, and it is the same with those beings about which I have been speaking and shall continue to speak in these lectures, the elemental beings of nature. Invisibly and supersensibly present behind what is physical and sense-perceptible, they participate in all the happenings of the world just as, or rather in a higher sense than do the physical, sense-perceptible beings.

Now you will readily be able to imagine that to these beings the world appears somewhat other than to the beings of the sense-world, for they do not possess a physical body such as is possessed by these latter. Everything which they grasp or perceive in the world must be different from what enters the human eye. This is indeed the case. The human being experiences the earth, for instance, as the cosmic body upon which he moves about. He even finds it slightly unpleasant when through some atmospheric condition or other, as occasionally occurs, this cosmic body becomes softened and he sinks into it even in a slight degree. He likes to feel the earth as something hard, as something into which he does not sink.

This whole way of experiencing things, this whole attitude towards the earth, is, however, completely alien to the gnomes; they sink down everywhere, because for them the whole earth-body is primarily a hollow space through which they can pass. They can penetrate everywhere; the rocks, the metals, present no hindrance to their—shall I say swimming around. There are no words in our language which really express this wandering about of the gnomes inside the body of the earth. It is just that they have an inner experience, an inner perception, of the different ingredients of the earth; when they wander along a vein of metal they have a different experience from when they take their way along a layer of chalk. All this, however, the gnomes feel inwardly, for through all such things they penetrate unhindered. They have not the least idea that the earth exists. Their idea is that there is a space within which they perceive certain experiences; the experience of gold, the experience of mercury, of tin, of silica, and so on. This is to express it in human language, not in the language of the gnomes. Their language is far more perceptive; and it is just because their whole life is spent in journeying along all the veins and seams—ever and again journeying along them—that they acquire the very pronounced intellectuality about which I have spoken to you. Through this they acquire their all-comprehensive knowledge, for in the metals and in the earth everything outside in the universe is revealed to them; as though in a mirror they experience everything which is outside in the universe. But for the earth itself the gnomes have no perception, only for its different constituents, and for the different kinds of inner experience which they offer.

Because of this the gnomes have a quite particular gift for receiving the impressions which come from the moon. It is towards the moon that they continually direct their attentive listening, and in this respect they are—I cannot say the born —it is so difficult to find the appropriate words—but the inherent neurasthenics. Of course, what for us is an illness is for these gnome-beings their actual life-element. For them this is no illness; it is simply a matter of course. It is what gives them that inner sensibility towards all those things of which I have spoken. But it also gives them their inner sensitivity towards the phenomena connected with the phases of the moon.

They follow the changes in the moon-phenomena with such close attention—I have already described their power of attention to you—that it actually alters their form. When, therefore, one follows the existence of a gnome, one receives quite a different impression at full moon from that one receives at new moon, and again at the intermediate phases.

At full moon the gnomes are ill at ease. Physical moon-light does not suit them, and at that time they thrust the whole feeling of their being outwards. They circumscribe themselves, as it were, with a spiritual skin. At full moon they press the feeling of their existence towards the boundary of their body. And in full moonlight, if one has imaginative perception for such things, they really appear like little shin-ing, mail-clad knights. They are clad in a kind of spiritual armour, and this it is which presses outwards in their skin to arm them against the moonlight which so displeases them. But when the time of new moon approaches the gnome be-comes transparent, wonderful to see, inwardly irradiated with a glittering play of colours. One sees within him, as it were, the processes of a whole world. It is as though one were to look into the human brain, not as an anatomist investigating the fabric of the cells, but as one who perceives inside the brain the shimmering and sparkling of the thoughts. That is how these transparent little folk, the gnomes, appear to one, as though the play of thoughts is revealed within them. It is just at new moon that the gnomes are so particularly interest-ing, for each of them bears a whole world within himself; and one can say that within this world there actually lies the mystery of the moon.

If one unveils it, this moon-mystery, one comes upon truly remarkable discoveries, for one reaches the conclusion that at the present time the moon is continually approaching nearer —naturally you must not take this in a crude way, as though the moon would collide with the earth—but each year it does in fact come somewhat nearer. Each year the moon is actu-ally nearer the earth. One recognises this from the ever more vigorous play of the moon-forces in the gnome-world during the time of the new moon. And to this coming nearer of the moon the attentiveness of these goblins is quite specially directed; for it is in producing results from the way in which the moon affects them that they see their chief mission in the universe. They await with intense expectation the epoch when the moon will again unite with the earth; and they assemble all their forces in order to be armed in readiness for the epoch when the moon will have united with the earth, for they will then use the moon substance gradually to disperse the earth, as far as its outer substance is concerned, into the universe. Its substance must pass away.

Because they hold this task in view these kobolds or gnomes feel themselves to be of quite special importance, for they gather together the most varied experiences from the whole of earth-existence, and they hold themselves in readiness, when all earthly substance will have been dispersed into the universe, —after the transition to the Jupiter-evolution—to preserve what is good in the structure of the earth in order to incorporate this in Jupiter as a kind of bony support.

You see, when one looks at this process from the aspect of the gnomes, one gains a first stimulus, a first capacity, to picture how our earth would appear if all the water were taken away from it. Just consider how, in the western hemisphere, everything is orientated from north to south, and how, in the eastern hemisphere, everything is orientated from east to west. Thus, if you were to do away with all the water, you would get in America, with its mountains and what lies under the sea, something which proceeds from north to south; and looking at Europe you would correspondingly find that, in the eastern hemisphere, the chain of the Alps, the Carpathians and so on, runs in the east-west direction. You would get something like the structure of the cross in the earth.

When one gains insight into this, one receives the impression that this is really the united gnome-world of the old Moon. The predecessors of our Earth-gnomes, the Moon-gnomes, gathered together their Moon-experiences and from them fashioned this structure, this firm structure of the solid fabric of the Earth, so that our solid Earth-structure actually arose from the experiences of the gnomes of the old Moon.

These are the things which reveal themselves in regard to the gnome-world. Through them the gnomes acquire an interesting, an extraordinarily interesting relationship to the

whole evolution of the universe. They always carry over the firm element of a preceding stage into the stage which follows. They are the preservers in evolution of the continuity of the firm structure, and thus they preserve the firm structure from one world-body to another. It belongs to the most interesting of studies to approach the supersensible world from the aspect of these spiritual beings and to observe their special task, for it is through this that one first gains an impression of how every kind of being existing in the world shares in the task of working upon the whole formation of the world.

Now let us pass over from the gnomes to the undines, the water-beings. Here a very remarkable picture presents itself. These beings have not the need for life that human beings have, neither have they the need for life that the animals have even though instinctively, but one could almost say that the undines, as also the sylphs, have rather a need for death. In a cosmic way they are really like the flying creature which casts itself into the flame. They only feel their life to be truly theirs when they die. This is extraordinarily interesting. Here on the physical earth everything desires to live, for all that has life-force in it is prized. It is the living, sprouting life that is valued. But once we have crossed the threshold, all these beings say to us that it is death which is really the true beginning of life. This can be felt by these beings. Let us take the undines. You know, perhaps, that sailors who travel a great deal on the sea find that in July, August and September—further to the west this is already the case in June—the Baltic Sea makes a peculiar impression, and they say that the sea is beginning to blossom. It becomes, as it were, productive; but it produces just those things which decay in the sea. The process of decay in the sea makes itself felt; it imparts to the sea a peculiar putrefactive smell.

All this, however, is different for the undines. It causes them no unpleasant sensations; but when the millions and millions of water-creatures which perish in the sea enter into the state of decomposition the sea becomes for the undines the most wonderful phosphorescent play of colours. It shines and glitters with every possible colour. Especially does the sea glitter for them, inwardly and outwardly, in every shade of blue, violet and green. The whole process of decomposition in the sea becomes a glimmering and gleaming of the darker colours up to the green. But these colours are realities for the undines, and one can see how, in this play of colours in the sea, they absorb the colours into themselves. They draw these colours into their own bodily nature. They become like them, they themselves become phosphorescent. And as they absorb the play of colours, as they themselves become phosphorescent, there arises in the undines something like a longing, an immense longing to rise upwards, to soar upwards. Upwards they soar, led by this longing, and with this longing they offer themselves to the beings of the higher hierarchies—to the angels, archangels and so on—as earthly sustenance; and in this sacrifice they find their bliss. Then within the higher hierarchies they live on further.

And thus we see the remarkable fact that each year with the return of early spring these beings evolve upwards from unfathomable depths. There they take part in the life of the earth by working on the plant-kingdom in the way I have described. Then, however, they pour themselves, as it were, into the water, and take up by means of their own bodily nature the phosphorescence of the water, the element of decomposition, and bear it upwards with an intensity of longing. Then in a vast, in a magnificent cosmic picture, one sees how, emanating from earthly water, the colours which are carried upwards by the undines and which have spiritual substantiality, provide the higher hierarchies with their sustenance, how the earth becomes the source of nourishment in that the very essence of the undines' longing is to let themselves be consumed by the higher beings. There they live on further; there they enter into their eternity. Thus every year there is a continual upstreaming of these undines, whose inner nature is formed out of the earthly sphere, and who radiate upwards, filled with the longing to offer themselves as nourishment to the higher beings.

And now let us proceed to the sylphs. In the course of the year we find the dying birds. I described to you how these dying birds possess spiritualized substance, and how they desire to give this spiritualized substance over to the higher worlds in order to release it from the earth. But here an intermediary is needed. And these intermediaries are the sylphs. It is a fact that through the dying bird-world the air is continually being filled with astrality. This astrality is of a lower order, but it is nevertheless astrality; it is astral substance. In this astrality flutter—or hover might be a better word—in this astrality hover the sylphs. They take up what comes from the dying bird-world, and carry it, again with a feeling of longing, up into the heights, only desiring to be inhaled by the beings of the higher hierarchies. They offer themselves as that which supplies breathing-existence to the higher hierarchies. Again a magnificent spectacle. With the dying bird-world, this astral, inwardly radiant substance is seen to pass over into the air. The sylphs flash like blue lightning through the air, and into their blue lightning, which assumes first greener, then redder tones, they absorb this astrality which comes from the bird-world, and dart upwards like upward-flashing lightning. And if one follows this beyond the boundaries of space, it becomes what is inhaled by the beings of the higher hierarchies.

Thus one can say : The gnomes carry one world over into another in regard to its structure. They progress, as it were in a direction—the expression is only used as a comparison—which is horizontal with evolution. The other beings—the undines, the sylphs—carry upwards what they experience as bliss in yielding themselves up to death, in being consumed, in being inhaled. There they continue to live within the higher hierarchies; within them they experience their eternity.

And when we pass over to the fire-beings, only think how the dust on the butterfly's wings seems to dissolve into nothing with the death of the butterfly. But it does not really dissolve into nothing. What is shed as dust from the butterfly's wings is the most highly spiritualized matter. And all this passes over like microscopic comets into the warmth-ether which surrounds the earth, each single particle of dust passes like a microscopic comet into the warmth-ether of the earth. When in the course of the year the butterfly-world approaches its end, all this becomes glittering and shimmering, an inner glittering and shimmering. And into this glittering and shimmering the fire-beings pour themselves; they absorb it. There it continues to glitter and shimmer, and they, too, get a feeling of longing. They bear what they have thus absorbed up into the heights. And now one sees—I have already described this to you from another aspect—how what the fire-beings carry outwards from the butterfly's wings shines forth into world-space. But it does not only shine forth; it streams forth. And it is this which provides the particular view of the earth, which is perceived by the higher hierarchies. The beings of the higher hierarchies gaze upon the earth, and what they principally see is this butterfly-and-insect-existence which has been carried outwards by the fire-beings; and the fire-beings find their highest ecstasy in the realization that it is they who present themselves before the spiritual eyes of the higher hierarchies. They find their highest bliss in being beheld by the gaze, by the spiritual eyes, of the higher hierarchies, in being absorbed into them. They strive upwards towards these beings and carry to them the knowledge of the earth.

Thus we see how these elemental beings are the intermediaries between the earth and the spirit-cosmos. We see this drama of the phosphorescent uprising of the undines, which pass away in the sea of light and flame of the higher hierarchies as their sustenance; we see the up-flashing of the greenish-reddish lightning, which is inbreathed there where the earth continually passes over into the eternal, the eternal survival of the fire-beings, whose activity never ceases. For whereas, here on earth, it is particularly at a certain time of the year that butterflies die, the fire-beings see to it that what it is their task to look to is poured out into the universe throughout the entire year. Thus the earth is as though cloaked in a mantle of fire. Seen from outside the earth appears fiery. But everything is brought about by beings who see the things of the earth quite differently from how man sees them. As already mentioned, man's experience of the earth is of a hard substance upon which he walks about and stands. For the gnomes it is a transparent globe, a hollow body. For the undines water is something in which they perceive the phosphorizing process, which they can take into themselves and feel as their life-element. Sylphs see in the astrality of the air, which emanates from dying birds, that which makes their lightning flashes more vivid than they would otherwise be, for in itself the lightning of these sylphs is dull and bluish. And then again the disintegration of butterfly existence is something which continually envelops the earth as though with a sheath of fire. When this is beheld it is as though the earth were surrounded by a wonderful fiery painting; and, on the other side, when one looks upwards from the earth, one beholds these lightning flashes, these phosphorescent and evanescent undines. All this makes us say: Here on earth the elemental nature-spirits live and weave; they strive upwards and pass away in the fire-mantle of the earth. In reality, however, they do not pass away, but there they find their eternal existence by passing over into the beings of the higher hierarchies.

All this, however, which at first appears like a wonderful world-picture is the expression of what happens on earth, for initially it is all played out upon the earth. We human beings are always present in what is there taking place; and the fact is—even if in his ordinary consciousness man is at first incapable of grasping what surrounds him—that every night we are involved in the weaving and working of these beings, that we ourselves take part as ego and as astral body in what these beings are carrying out.

But it is the gnomes especially which really find it quite an entertainment to observe a person who is asleep, not the physical body in bed, but the person who is outside his physical body in his astral body and ego, for what the gnome sees is someone who thinks in the spirit but does not know it. He does not know that his thoughts live in the spiritual. And again for the undines it is inexplicable that man knows himself so little; likewise with the sylphs, and likewise with the fire-beings.

On the physical plane, you see, it is certainly often unpleasant to have gnats and the like buzzing around one at night. But the spiritual man, the ego and astral body—at night these are surrounded and woven about by elemental beings; and this being surrounded and woven about is a constant admonition to man to give an impetus to his consciousness in order to know more about the world.

Now, therefore, I can try to give you an idea of what these beings—gnomes, undines, sylphs and fire-beings—mean with their buzzing about, of what happens when we begin to hear what amuses them in us, and of what they would have us do when they admonish us to give a forward impetus to our consciousness. Yes, you see, here come the gnomes and speak somewhat as follows :

> You dream your self,
> And shun awakening.

The gnomes know that man possesses his ego as though in a dream, that he must first awaken in order to arrive at his true ego. They see this quite clearly, and call to him in his sleep :

> You dream your self

—they mean during the day—

> And shun awakening.

Then there sounds forth from the undines :

> You think the deeds of angels

Man does not know that his thoughts are really with the angels

> You think the deeds of Angels
> And know it not.

And from the sylphs there sounds to sleeping man :

> Creative Might shines to you,
> You divine it not.
> You feel its strength

—the strength of Creative Might—

> And live it not.

Such approximately are the words of the sylphs, the words of the undines, the words of the gnomes.

The words of the fire-beings :

> Divine Will offers you strength,
> You accept it not.
> With its strength you will,

—with the strength of Divine Will—

> Yet thrust it from you.

The aim of all these admonitions is to give man a forward impetus in regard to his consciousness. These beings, which do not enter into physical existence, wish man to make a move onward with his consciousness, so that he, too, may participate in their world.

And when one has thus entered into what these beings have to say to man, one also gradually understands how they give expression to their own nature, somewhat in this way:

The gnomes:

> I maintain the life-force in the root,
> It creates for me my body's form.

The undines:

> I bestir the water's power of growth,
> It forms for me substance of life.

The sylphs:

> I quaff the airy force of life,
> It fills me with the power of being.

And the fire-beings—there it is very difficult to find any kind of earthly words for what they do, because their sphere is far removed from earthly life and earthly activity.

Fire-beings:

> I consume* the striving power of fire,
> Into soul-spirit it releases me.

You see, I have endeavoured to the best of my ability to give you an idea of how these beings of the elemental kingdom characterize themselves; and of the admonitions which they impart to man. But they are not so unfriendly to man as only to suggest to him what is negative in its nature, but pithy and

---

* Here Rudolf Steiner coins a word from verdauen, to digest: däuen—ich däue, to express, not ordinary digestion, but a fiery consuming process.

positive sayings also proceed from them. And man experiences these sayings as being of immense, of gigantic import.
In such matters as these you must acquire a sense for whether
a saying is uttered merely in human words, however beautiful
they may be, or whether it sounds forth as though cosmically
from the whole mighty chorus of the gnomes. It is the whole
manner of its arising which brings about the difference. And
when man hearkens to the gnomes after the admonitions
which I have written down have been imparted to him, then
there sounds towards him from the massed chorus of the
gnomes:

> Strive to awaken.

Here the significance is the mighty moral impression created
by such words when they stream through the universe, arising
from the massed chorus of infinitely many single voices.

And from the undine chorus resounds:

> Think in the spirit.

With the chorus of sylphs things are not so simple. When the
gnomes appear like shining armoured knights in full moon-
light there resounds from them as though from earth-depths:

> Strive to awaken.

When the undines soar upwards filled with the longing to be
consumed, then in this upsoaring there sounds back to the
earth:

> Think in the Spirit.

But for the sylphs, in that, up above, they allow themselves to
be inhaled, disappearing in bluish-reddish-greenish lightning
into the world-light, then, as they flash into the light and there-
in disappear, from the heights there sounds down from them:

> Live creatively breathing existence.

And as in fiery anger—but anger which is not felt to be anni-
hilating, but rather as something which man must receive
from the cosmos—as in fiery but at the same time enthusiastic

anger, the fire-beings carry what is theirs into the fire-mantle of the earth, their words resound. Here the sound is not like that of single voices massed together, but from the whole circumference there resounds as with a mighty voice of thunder :

Receive in love the Will-Force of the Gods.

Naturally, one can turn one's attention away from all this; then one does not perceive it. Whether or no man does perceive such things depends upon his own free decision. But when man does perceive them he knows that they are an integral part of cosmic existence, that something actually occurs in that gnomes, undines, sylphs and fire-beings unfold their evolution in the way described. And the gnomes are not only present for man in the way I have already portrayed, but they are there to let their world-words sound forth from the earth, the undines to let their world-words soar upwards, the sylphs theirs from above, the fire-beings theirs like a chorus, like the massing of a mighty uplifting of voices.

Yes, this is how it could appear when transposed into words. But these words belong to the Word of worlds, and even though we do not hear them with ordinary consciousness, these words are yet not without significance for mankind. For the primeval idea which had its source in instinctive clair-voyance, that the world was born out of the Word, is indeed a profound truth, but the world-word is not some collection of syllables gathered from here or there; the world-word is what sounds forth from countless, countless beings. Countless, countless beings have something to say in the totality of the world, and the world-word sounds forth from the concordance of these countless beings. It is not the general abstract truth that the world is born out of the Word that can bring this to us in its fullness. One thing alone can do this, namely that we gradually arrive at a concrete understanding ow how the world-word in all its different nuances is composed of the voices of individual beings, so that these different nuances contribute their sound, their utterance, to the great world-harmony, the mighty world-melody, in the Word's act of *creation*.

When the gnome-chorus allows its "Strive to awaken" to sound forth, this—only transformed into gnome-language—is the force which is active in bringing about the human bony system, the system of movement in general.

When the undines utter "Think in the spirit", they utter—transposed into the undine-sphere—what pours itself as world-word into man in order to give form to the organs of digestion.

When the sylphs, as they are breathed in, allow their "Live creatively breathing existence" to stream downwards, there penetrates into man, weaving and pulsating through him, the force which endows him with the organs of the rhythmic system.

And if one attends to what sounds inwardly—in the manner of the fire-beings—from the fire-mantle of the world, then one finds that this sounding manifests as image or reflection. It streams in from the fire-mantle—this sounding force of the word. And every nerve system of every man, every head I would add, is a miniature image of what—translated into the language of the fire-beings—rings out as : "Receive in love the Will-Power of the Gods". This saying, "Receive in love the Will-Power of the Gods", this is what is active in the highest substance of the world. And when man is experiencing his development in the life between death and a new birth, this it is which transforms what he brought with him through the gate of death into what will later become the human organs of the nerves and senses. So we have :

	System of movement
Chorus of gnomes :	Strive to awaken
	Metabolic organization
Undines :	Think in the Spirit
	Rhythmic system
Sylphs :	Live creatively breathing existence.
	Nerve-senses system
Fire-beings :	Receive in love the Will-Power of the Gods.

Thus you see that what lies beyond the threshold is akin to our own nature, you see how it leads us into the creative divine forces, into what lives and works in all forms of existence. And when one calls to mind what an earlier epoch divined, and is expressed in the words:

> The power of life, the seeds behold;
> Turn thee away from words' cramped mould.*

—one is impelled to say that all this must become actuality in the further course of the development of mankind. We cramp all knowledge into words if we have no insight into the germinating forces which build up the human being in the most varied ways.

We can therefore say that the system of movement, the metabolic system, the rhythmic system, the system of nerves and senses merge into a unity in that they resound in harmony. For there sounds upwards from below: "Strive to awaken"; "Think in the Spirit"—and from above downwards, mingling with the upward-striving words, "Live creatively breathing existence"; "Receive in love the Will-Power of the Gods".

This "Receive in love the Will-Power of the Gods" is the calm creative element in the head. Then what strives from below upwards in "Think in the Spirit", from above downwards in "Live creatively breathing existence", in their combined activity is what so works and weaves that it creates an image of the way in which human breathing passes over in a rhythmical way into the activity of the blood. And what implants into us the instruments of the senses, this is what streams from above downwards in "Receive in love the Will-Power of the Gods". But what works in our walking, in our standing, in our moving of the arms and hands, everything in fact which brings man into the manifestation of his element of will, this sounds forth in "Strive to awaken".

Thus you see how man is a symphony of that world-word which can be interpreted on its lowest level in the way I have

* Goethe: *Faust*, Part I, Scene I.

presented it to you. Then this world-word ascends to the higher hierarchies, whose task it is to unfold other aspects of this world-word in order that the cosmos may arise and develop. But that which has, as it were, been uttered as a call into the world by these elemental beings is the final reverberation of that creative, upbuilding, form-giving world-word which lies at the base of all activity and all existence.

Gnomes	You dream your Self,
	And shun awakening.
	I maintain the life-force in the root,
	It creates for me my body's form.
Undines	You think the deeds of Angels
	And know it not.
	I bestir the water's power of growth,
	It forms for me substance of life.
Sylphs	Creative might shines to you,
	You divine it not;
	You feel its strength
	And live it not.
	I quaff the airy force of life,
	It fills me with the power of being.
Fire-beings	Divine Will offers you strength,
	You accept it not.
	With its strength you will,
	Yet thrust it off from you.
	I consume the striving power of fire,
	Into soul-spirit it releases me.
Chorus of gnomes	Strive to awaken!
Undines	Think in the Spirit!
Sylphs	Live creatively breathing existence!
Fire-beings	Receive in love the Will-Power of the Gods!

Gnomen Du träumst dich selbst,
    Und meidest das Erwachen.

    Ich halte die Wurzelwesenskraft,
    Sie schaffet mir den Formenleib.

Undinen Du denkst die Engelwerke,
    Und weisst es nicht.

    Ich bewege die Wasserwachstumskraft,
    Sie bildet mir den Lebensstoff.

Sylphen Dir leuchtet die Schöpfermacht,
    Du ahnst es nicht,
    Du fühlest ihre Kraft,
    Und lebst sie nicht.

    Ich schlürfe die luft'ge Lebekraft,
    Sie füllet mich mit Seinsgewalt.

Feuerwesen Dir kraftet Götterwille,
    Du empfängst ihn nicht.
    Du willst mit seiner Kraft
    Und stossest ihn von dir.

    Ich däue die Feuerstrebekraft,
    Sie erlöst mich in Seelengeistigkeit.

Gnomenchor Erstrebe zu wachen!

Undinen Denke im Geiste!

Sylphen Lebe schaffend atmendes Dasein!

Feuerwesen Empfange liebend Götterwillenskraft!

Part Four

The Secrets of the Human Organism

Physical natural laws, etheric natural laws, are the characters of a script which depicts the spiritual world. We only understand these things when we are able to conceive them as written characters from spiritual worlds.

LECTURE X

9th November, 1923

In the lectures which I have given recently you will have seen that everything was directed towards so bringing together world-phenomena that eventually a really comprehensive knowledge of man might result. Everything we have been studying here has had the knowledge of man as its goal. Such a knowledge of man will only become possible when it begins with the lowest forms of the world of phenomena and relates them to everything that is revealed to man as the material world. But what begins in this way with the study of the entire world of matter must end with the study of the world of the hierarchies. It is in proceeding from the lowest forms of material up to the highest forms of spiritual existence that we must seek to discover what will eventually lead to a true knowledge of man. For the present we will use the lectures I am now able to give you to make a kind of sketch of such a knowledge of man.

We must be quite clear about the fact that what we now recognise as man is a product of that long cosmic evolution which I have always synthesized as the Saturn-Sun-Moon-and-Earth-evolution. The Earth-evolution is not yet completed. But let us be clear about what man owes to this Earth-evolution in the narrower sense, to the epoch, that is to say, which is subsequent to the evolution of old Moon. You see, when you move your arms and stretch them out, when you move your fingers, when you carry out any kind of external movement, everything in your organism which enables you to move your arms and legs, your head, your lips, and so on—and the forces upon which man's external movements depend enter into the most inward parts of the human organism—all this was vouchsafed to man by Earth-evolution in the narrower sense. If, on the other hand, you look into everything connected with the development of the metabolism, which is enclosed by man's outer skin, if you look at all the metabolic functions within the physical body, here you have a picture of what man owes to the Moon-evolution. And you have a picture of what man owes to the old Sun-evolution when you look into everything within him which involves some kind of rhythmic process. Breathing and blood-circulation are of course the most important of these rhythmic processes, and these man owes to the old Sun-evolution. Everything comprised in the system of nerves and senses, which in men of today is distributed over the whole body, this man owes to the old Saturn-evolution.

In regard to all this, however, you must bear in mind that the human being is a whole and that world-evolution is a whole. When today we draw attention to the old Saturn-evolution in the way I did in my "Occult Science", we mean the period of evolution previous to the primordial epochs of the Sun-Moon-and-Earth-evolution. But this is only one Saturn-evolution, that from which the Earth resulted. But during the period in which the Earth was evolving, a Saturn-evolution also came into being. This Saturn-evolution is included in the Earth-evolution; it is, so to speak, the youngest Saturn-evolution. The one that did not reach the Earth-evolution is the oldest. The Saturn-evolution which was inserted into old Sun is younger; the one inserted into old Moon is younger still. And the Saturn which today imbues the Earth, and is actually responsible for certain aspects of its warmth-organization, this Saturn is the youngest of all. We, with our human nature, are a part of this Saturn-evolution.

Thus are we placed into cosmic evolution. But we are also placed into what surrounds us spacially on the earth. Take, for example, the mineral kingdom. We live in a state of reciprocal action with the mineral kingdom. We take the mineral element into ourselves through our food. We absorb it in other ways, too, through our breathing, and so on. We assimilate the mineral element.

But all evolution, all world-processes, are different within man from what they are outside him. I have already mentioned that it is a real absurdity when people today study chemical processes in laboratories, and then think that when a person eats certain foodstuffs these processes will simply continue inside him. Man is not some kind of confluence of chemical actions; inside him everything is altered. And from a certain standpoint this alteration appears in the following way.

Let us suppose that we take into ourselves something of a mineral nature. Every such mineral substance must be so far worked upon within the human being that the following result is brought about. You know that we have our own individual temperature; in the healthy person this is about 98° Fahrenheit (37° centigrade). In the warmth of our blood we have something which exceeds the warmth outside us. Everything which we take in as mineral substance must, however, be so transformed, so metamorphosed in our organism that, where the warmth of our blood exceeds the average warmth of its external environment, where it rises above the average external warmth of our surroundings, this excess of warmth absorbs with satisfaction the mineral element within us. If you eat a grain of cooking-salt, this grain of salt must be absorbed by your individual warmth, not by the warmth which you have in common with the outside world. It must be absorbed with satisfaction by your own individual warmth. Everything mineral must be transformed into warmth-ether. And the moment a person has something in his organism which prevents any kind of mineral from being changed into warmth-ether, at that moment he is ill.

Now let us proceed to the plant-substances which man takes into himself. Man takes in plant-substances; he, too, belongs to the plant kingdom inasmuch as he develops the plant-element within himself. He contains what is of a mineral nature; this, however, continually has the tendency to become warmth-ether. The plant element continually has the tendency

in man to become airy, to become gaseous. So that man has
the plant element within himself in its aspect of air. Everything of a plant nature which enters man, or whatever he himself develops as inner plant organisation, must become airy,
must be able to assume the form of air within him. If it does
not assume the form of air, if his organization is such that it
hinders him from letting what is of a plant-nature within him
pass over into the form of air, he becomes ill. Everything of
animal-nature which man takes in or develops within himself
must—in time at least—assume the fluid, the watery form.
Man may not have what is of an animal nature within him,
whether inwardly produced or absorbed from outside, unless
at some time it submits to the process of becoming fluid. If
man is not in a position to liquidize either his own or foreign
animal substance so as to transform it further into the solid,
then he becomes ill. Only that in man which is indigenous to
the purely human form, which arises from his nature as a
being who walks upright, having within him the impulses to
speak and think, only that which gives man his real humanity,
which raises him above the animal—and this is at most a
tenth of his whole organism—may enter into solid formation,
into actual form. If anything of animal or plant nature
invades the human solid form, man is ill.

Everything mineral must eventually become warmth-ether
in man. Everything vegetable must undergo a transitional airy
stage in man. Everything animal must pass through an intermediate watery stage in man. Only what is human may always
retain within itself the earthly-solid form. This is one of the
secrets of the human organization.

And now to begin with let us leave aside everything that
man has from the Earth-epoch—thereby making our further
studies of this all the more fruitful—and let us take the metabolic system as such, which, though certainly developed as an
Earth-organization, nevertheless received its germinal beginnings from the epoch of old Moon. Let us therefore take
digestion in the narrower sense of what takes place inside the
human skin—in which we must of course include the excre-

tory processes—and we shall find that all substances become altered in the intake of food. The food-substances, which at first are outside man, enter into him, and merge themselves with the digestive system. This digestive system now converts what belonged to man's surroundings into what is essentially human. Everything mineral begins to assume the condition of warmth-ether, everything vegetable the gaseous-airy-vaporous condition, everything animal, including what is self-produced, begins to assume the fluid condition; and all begin to build what is now essentially human into a firmly organized structural form. All this is inherent in digestion. And digestion is consequently something of remarkable interest.

If we ascend from digestion to breathing, we notice that man produces carbon out of himself, and that this is to be found everywhere within him. This is sought out by oxygen, becomes changed into carbonic acid, and is then exhaled. Carbonic acid is the combination of carbon and oxygen. The oxygen, which is drawn in through breathing, masters the carbon, absorbs the carbon into itself; carbonic acid, the product of oxygen and carbon, is then exhaled. But before exhalation occurs, the carbon becomes the benefactor, so to speak, of human nature. This carbon—in that it combines with the oxygen, in that it combines to a certain extent what the blood-circulation brings about with what the breathing produces—this carbon becomes the benefactor of the human organization, for, before it leaves the human organization, it disperses through it an outstreaming of ether. Physical science merely states that carbon is exhaled with carbonic acid. This, however, is only one side of the whole process. Man exhales the carbonic acid; but in the process of this exhalation something of the carbon taken up by the oxygen is left behind in his whole organism, namely ether. This ether penetrates into man's etheric body, and it is this ether, continually being produced by the carbon, which makes the human organization capable of opening itself to spiritual influences, of absorbing astral-etheric forces from the cosmos. This ether, which is left behind by the carbon, attracts the cosmic impulses, and they in their turn work formatively upon man, so preparing his nervous system, for instance, that it can become the bearer of thoughts. This ether must continually permeate our senses, our eyes, for example, so that they may see, so that they may receive the outer light-ether. Thus we are indebted to carbon for the supply of ether within us which enables us to come into contact with the outer world.

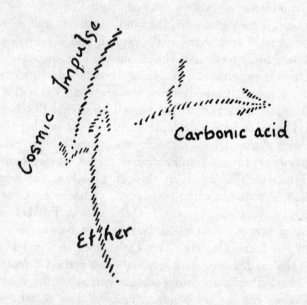

All this is already prepared in the metabolic system. But the metabolism as a human system is so placed into the whole cosmos that it could not exist for itself alone. Isolated in itself the digestive system could not exist. This is why it was the third system to have its rudiments implanted in man. The rudiments of the system of nerves and senses took form in the epoch of old Saturn; the second system, the rhythmic system, was laid down during the epoch of old Sun. Only after these other systems had come into being could the metabolic system be produced, because in and for itself this system could not exist. The metabolic system, if at first we omit its involuntary movements, is intended, in its cosmic connection, to provide for human nutrition. But these processes of nutrition cannot function independently. Digestion is necessary to man, but in and for itself it cannot exist. For if we study the human metabolic system in isolation—in the forthcoming lectures you will again see how necessary it is for the whole human organism—we find it constantly imbued with every kind of tendency towards illness. And the origin of internal illnesses—not those caused by external injury—must always be looked for in the metabolic system. Anyone, therefore, who wishes to put forward a rational observation of illness must start with the metabolic system; and in regard to every metabolic phenomenon he must really ask: Now where did you come from? When we consider all the phenomena, from the taking of food into the mouth, from the way the food is worked upon so that we transform certain substances into starch, sugar and so on, when we take the enveloping action of ptyalin in the mouth, when we go further and take the pepsin process in the stomach, and the assimilation of the products in digestion, following all these as far as their passage into the lymphatic vessels and into the blood—then we realize that each single one of these processes must be investigated—and their number is legion. The mingling of the products of digestion with the secretions of the pancreatic glands, the further mingling of these substances with the secretions from the gall-bladder, and so on—to each single process the question must be put: What is it that you really want? And it will answer: If I am alone I am a process which always makes man ill. No digestive process in human nature may be carried to its conclusion, for every digestive process which is carried to its conclusion makes man ill. The human constitution is only healthy when the metabolic processes are checked at a certain stage.

It might at first seem a folly in world-organization that something should begin in man which, if not checked halfway, would make him ill; but in the next lectures we shall learn to recognize this as something of the utmost wisdom. For the time being, however, let us study the actual facts, and discover what the answer of the separate digestive processes would be if we were to question their inner nature. We are always on the way to making our whole organism ill. Every digestive process, if unchecked, causes illness in the organism. If, therefore, digestion is to exist at all in man, other processes must exist whose germinal beginnings date from earlier times. These are the processes which are present in circulation, the circulatory processes. The circulation continually produces the processes of healing. So that we may really describe the human being by saying: During the old Moon evolution man was born as patient, and the doctor within him was already sent in advance during the epoch of old Sun. In regard to his own organism man was already born as doctor during the evolution of old Sun. It shows great foresight on the part of world-evolution that the doctor came into existence before the patient, for the patient in man himself was only added on old Moon. And if we are to describe man rightly, we must work backwards from the digestive to the circulatory processes, including, of course, all those impulses which underlie the circulatory system. Speaking broadly one substance induces quicker, another substance slower circulation. We have also quite small circulatory processes within us. Take any mineral substance, gold, let us say, or copper. Every such substance when induced into man—by the mouth, by injection, or in any other way—is endowed with the power of causing something to be formed or altered in the circulation, so as to work in a curative way, and so on. And what one must know, in order to gain insight into the essential healing processes in man, is what each single substance in his world-environment releases in man through alterations in his circulation. Thus one may say that circulation is a continual process of healing.

You can if you wish work this out for yourselves. Recall how I told you that on an average man draws eighteen breaths a minute. Here we find a remarkably regular agreement with the cosmos, for the number of breaths man draws in a day equals the number of circulatory rhythms carried out by the sun in its course through the solar year. As regards its rising point at the vernal equinox the sun traverses the entire zodiac in the course of 25,920 years. In middle life man draws on an average 25,920 breaths a day. The pulse-beats are four times as many. The other circulation, the circulation which is concentrated more inwardly, is influenced by the digestion. Breath-circulation brings man into outer intercourse with the surrounding world, into reciprocal relationship with it. This breath-rhythm must continually restrain the rhythm of blood-circulation, so that it remains in its proportion of one to four, otherwise man would come into a quite irregular rhythm, reaching the number 103,680. This corresponds to nothing in the cosmos; it would completely sever man and cosmos. His digestion tears him out of the cosmos, estranges him from the cosmos; the rhythm of his breathing continually pulls him back into it. In this holding the rhythm of circulation in control by the rhythm of breathing, you see the primal healing process which is continually at work in man. In a certain delicate way, in the case of every internal cure, we must assist the breathing process, continued as it is into the whole body, and this in such a manner that everywhere in the human being the process of circulation is held in control, is brought back into the general relationships of the cosmos.

Thus we may say : We pass over from nutrition to healing inasmuch as from below upwards man always has the tendency to become ill, and therefore in his central organism, in his organism of circulation, he must continually develop the tendency to remain well. And in that in our central organism healing impulses continually arise, they leave something behind in the head-nerve-senses system. Thus we are brought to the third part of our organism, the system of nerves and senses.

What kind of forces do we find in the nerve-senses system? We find those forces which, so to speak, the doctor in us leaves behind. On the one hand he works down into the metabolism in a health-giving way. But through this curative working upon the digestive process he actually does something which affects the whole cosmos. What I am saying is nothing fantastic, but an absolute reality. This process, which continually works downwards in us in a healing way, calls forth a feeling of pleasure in the higher hierarchies. It constitutes the joy of the higher hierarchies in the earthly world. They look down and continually feel the uprising of illness out of what streams upwards in man from the earthly, from what remains of the earthly attributes of the substances. And they also see how the forces which work away from the earthly, the forces which lie in the encircling air, and the like, are continually active as processes of healing. This arouses satisfaction in the higher hierarchies.

And now try to gain an idea of what may be studied in regard to that cosmic body which, as the spiritual object most deserving of study, is situated at the outer boundary of our planetary system. In the centre of this body we find those forces concealed which, if you think of them as concentrated upon the earth, are the illness inducing forces, and surrounding this same body the encircling forces reveal themselves as the forces which bring about healing. Anyone sensitive to such things will see encircling health in the rings of Saturn, and this in a more distinct way than it can be perceived in what surrounds the earth, because there we stand in the midst of it. A Saturn ring is something essentially different from what astronomers have to say about it. It is encircling health, whereas the inner part of Saturn develops illness; it is the illness-inducing element seen in its most radical concentration.

Thus we see in Saturn, which is situated at the outermost boundary of our planetary system, the very same process at work which we continually bear within ourselves through our digestive and circulatory organism. But we also find, when we look at all this, that our spiritual gaze is directed further to the worlds of the first and second hierarchy, to the beings of the second hierarchy, Kyriotetes, Exusiai, Dynamis, and to the beings of the first hierarchy, Seraphim, Cherubim, Thrones. If with our spiritual eye we are attentive to Saturn and its ring, we shall be led to these upper hierarchies, as they survey with satisfaction the illness-inducing and health-restoring processes.

And this satisfaction is in itself a force in the universe. It streams through our system of nerves and senses and forms within it the forces of the spiritual evolution of mankind. These are the forces which blossom forth, as it were, from the healing-process which is continually at work in man. Thus in the third place we have the forces of spiritual evolution.

1.	Digestion	Nutrition
2.	Circulation	Healing
3.	System of nerves and senses	Spiritual evolution.

And if we now describe man in the epochs of Saturn, Sun and Moon, we must say : In the first place man is born out of the cosmos as spirit, he then develops within himself the "healer", and thus enables himself to deal with the cosmic "patient". And through the interworking of all these activities man came into being upon the earth possessed of full freedom of movement.

Every single branch of human knowledge must in a certain sense be inspired by what I have said here. Let us suppose that someone wishes to found a system of healing, a really rational system of healing. What would this have to contain? In the first place, naturally, the processes of healing. But these healing-processes, from where must they take their start? They must take their start from the metabolic processes; and everything else can at most be supposition—we shall have something further to say about this later—anatomy too, even in a delicate form, can at most be a starting point, because it is concerned with the formed and solid. This immediately expresses the human element. But it is the digestive processes which must be studied in the first place by a rational system of medicine, and this in such a way that one always perceives in them tendencies leading towards the inducement of illness. A modern system of medicine must always take the metabolic system, that is to say the normal processes of digestion, as its point of departure; and starting from there it must deduce how internal illnesses, in the widest sense, can arise from the metabolism. Then, through an intimate knowledge of the action of the rhythmic processes, the true nature of therapy must be discovered. A modern system of medicine must, therefore, be founded on a study of the metabolic processes, and then, from this initial study, the transition must be made to everything which can make its appearance in the sphere of the rhythmic processes in man. Further, a kind of crowning of the whole will be attained in that one shows how a sound development of man's spiritual possibilities presupposes a knowledge of what arises from the healing forces. Today you will find no true pedagogy—no art, that is to say, of the sound development of man's spiritual nature—if you do not take your start from the processes of healing; for these healing processes are nothing other than applying to the central nature of the human being what must already be made use of in pure thinking when developing the spiritual processes of man.

The artist in education must work in a spiritual way with the forces which, whether concentrated in the physical or concentrated in the etheric, are processes of healing. Whatever I may do to a child in the sphere of education is a process which has something spiritual as its basis. If I transpose this process, so that what was an activity in the spirit I now carry out in such a way that I make use of some kind of substance or physical process, then this process or substance becomes a remedy. So that it may really be said that medicine is the treatment of man in the spiritual sphere metamorphosed downwards into the sphere of the material. If you call to mind the way in which I dealt with things in the teachers' course held some time back for English visitors,* you will see how I everywhere drew attention to the fact that the work of the teacher is the beginning of a kind of general therapy, and I showed how this or that set of educational ideas can be the initial cause of unhealthy conditions in the excretory processes or of digestive irregularities in later life. So that what the teacher does, projected downwards, gives us therapy. And the antithesis of this therapy—what works from below upwards—this is brought about by the process of digestion.

Here you also see why a system of medicine today must be born out of a knowledge of man as a whole. And this is possible. Many people feel it. But nothing can really be achieved until such a system of medicine is actually developed. Today this must be counted among the most urgent of necessities. If you look at modern text-books of medicine, you will see that, with the rarest exceptions, they do not take their start from the metabolic system. But this must be the point of departure, otherwise one does not learn to know the real nature of illness.

You see, the whole matter proceeds in such a way that the processes of human nutrition can pass over into processes of healing, these again into spiritual processes; and, working backwards, spiritual processes can pass over into healing processes. If, on the other hand, spiritual processes are the direct cause of digestive disturbances, these spiritual processes must again enter into a condition in which they must be cured by the central system of man. All these things pass one into the other in man, and the whole human organization is an example of continual and wonderful metamorphosis. Take, for example, the processes inherent in the whole marvellous cir-

* See *Lectures to Teachers*, a report by Albert Steffen.

culation of the human blood. What kind of processes are these?

To begin with, separating it entirely from the rest of the organism, let us gain an idea of the human blood, how it flows through the veins; and let us consider the human form, the system of veins, the muscular system in its connection with the bony system, all the solid structure of the body and what flows through it as fluid. And first let us confine ourselves in the fluid condition to the blood. There are, of course, other fluids present, but let us confine ourselves to the blood. Now what are the processes which are continually happening in this streaming fluidity? These processes in the flowing blood can seize hold, in one direction or another, on the walls of the organs, on the bony structure, on anything which can take on a solid formation in man: then what belongs to the blood enters into the walls of the vessels, into the muscles, into one or another of the bones, or into any containing organ. What does it become there? It becomes the impulse towards inflammatory conditions.

What we find here or there as impulses towards inflammatory conditions is continually to be found as normal processes in the flowing blood. What appears as inflammation is something in the wrong place; that is to say processes which must always be present in the fluid blood have trespassed into the solid structure. A perfectly healthy normal process, displaced, transferred to another situation where it does not belong, becomes a process which induces illness. And certain illnesses of the nervous system consist just in this, that the nervous system, which in its whole organization is the polar opposite of the blood-system, is subjected to invasion by processes which are normal in the blood. If these processes which are normal in the blood-channels invade the paths of the nerves even in the slightest degree, then the nerves are attacked by inflammation in its initial stages; and this can develop into the most diverse forms of illness in the nervous system.

I mentioned that the processes in the blood are entirely different from those in the nerves; they are the antithesis of each other. In the blood-processes the urge is towards the phosphorizing element. When these phosphorizing processes take hold of what encloses or is adjacent to the blood, they lead to inflammatory conditions. But if the processes in the paths of the nerves themselves deviate into the adjacent organs and even into the blood, then impulses towards every kind of swelling arise in man. When these processes are carried over into the blood so that they affect the other organs in an unhealthy way, the formation of swellings or tumours makes its appearance. Every swelling or tumour is a metamorphosed nerve-process wrongly situated in the human organism.

What has its course in the nerve must remain in the nerve, and what has its course in the blood must remain in the blood. If what belongs in the blood trespasses into what is adjacent to it, inflammatory conditions arise. When what belongs in the nerve trespasses into what is adjacent to it, all kinds of formations arise which can be grouped together under the designation of swelling-formations. The aim must be to establish the correct rhythm between the processes in the nervous system and the processes in the system of the blood.

Not only have we in general the rhythm of breathing contrasted with the rhythm of the blood, but we have delicate processes in the circulation of the blood, which, when they depart from the blood, become the causes of inflammation. These delicate processes must also enter into a certain rhythmic connection with what is proceeding in the adjacent nerves, just as breathing must stand in a certain connection with the circulation of the blood. And the moment something is disturbed between blood-rhythm and nerve-rhythm it must once more be brought into adjustment.

Here again, you see, we come into the domain of therapy, of healing. All this serves to show you how everything must be present in man, how above all an element of illness must be present so that in another situation it may become an element of health; it has only been brought into the wrong situation through an incorrect process. For if it were not there at all man could not exist. Man could not exist if he were unable to get inflammations, for the inflammation-inducing forces must continually be present in the blood. This was my meaning when I often said that everything one gains in the way of knowledge must be won from a real *knowledge of man*. Here you see the reasons why an education carried out in an up-in-the-air, abstract fashion is really something absurd. Education must in fact be so carried out that everywhere the start is taken from certain pathological processes in man, and from the possibility of curing them.

If one understands a brain-illness and the means by which brain-illnesses may be cured, then, to put things bluntly— from a certain point of view this is of course also a subtle matter, but I put it "bluntly" because we are dealing with a physical process—then, in the treatment of the brain, we are concerned precisely with what must be applied in the art of education. It is therefore the case that, if we ever came actually to founding a training college for teachers we should have to introduce the pathological-therapeutical aspect to the teachers, and here their thinking should be schooled by means of more perceptible things, because these are more rooted in the material, so preparing them to grasp things concerned with actual education. On the other hand, nothing is of greater assistance in therapy, particularly in the treatment of internal illnesses, than to know the effect produced by the way in which this or that aspect of the art of education is handled. For if one finds the bridge from this to the material, then, from the very way in which one should act in education, the remedy is also to be found.

If, for example, one discovers the right educational means of treating certain lethargic conditions in the children, arising from certain disturbances in the metabolic system, one develops quite remarkable inner faculties. It is necessary, of course, really to immerse oneself in the education, and not have such an external approach that, when school is over, one prefers to spend all the evening in a convivial club and forget all about what happens in the classroom. From the very way one handles a lethargic child one gains the faculty to perceive the whole working of the head-processes, and their relation to the processes of the abdomen. And further, when in mineralogy one studies the processes which take place in copper when it gives rise to this or that formation in the earth, then what copper does in becoming one or another kind of copper ore makes one say to oneself: The copper-force in the earth actually does what you as teacher do with a boy or a girl! In what is accomplished by copper one sees an image of what one carries out oneself. And it is extraordinarily fascinating for a teacher to develop an instinctive, an intuitive clarity of feeling in regard to what he himself does, and then to have the delight of going out into nature in order to see what nature accomplishes in the way of education on an immense scale. There he may see, for example, how, wherever harmful results might ensue from some lime-process, a copper-process is introduced into it. Yes, in these copper-processes, in these ore-forming processes, which have their place within the other processes of the earth, remedial effects are continually present. If somewhere or other one finds pyrite-ores, or the like, it is fascinating to be able to say: Yes, this is exactly the same as when a patient receives the right treatment. But here the treatment is accomplished by the spirits of nature, from the hierarchies down to those elemental spirits about which I have spoken to you, in their capacity as healers of all the destructive, illness-inducing processes which can appear in life. This is in fact nothing more than reading from nature. For if one sees what is happening outside, if one accepts this or that substance as a remedy or prepares it as such, one has only to ask oneself: Where do the foodstuffs grow? Where does this or that metal appear in the veins of the earth? Study their environment and you will always find that, wherever some form of metal appears here or there, which has been dealt with by nature in one or another way, a remedial process is at work within it. Only appropriate this and continue it on into the human organism and you will create a therapy which nature has demonstrated to you in the world outside.

Yes, all the goings-on of the world are in reality a true education in all questions of nutrition, of healing, of the spiritual; for in nature illness is continually being induced and is continually being cured. They are there outside, the great cosmic processes of healing. We must only apply them to man. This is the wonderful interworking of the macrocosm with the microcosm. What I have said to many of you in one context or another is profoundly true:

> Willst du dich selber erkennen,
> Blicke in die Welt nach allen Seiten.
> Willst du die Welt erkennen,
> Schaue in alle deine eigenen Tiefen.

> Wouldst thou know thyself,
> Look into the world on every side.
> Wouldst thou know the world,
> Look into the depths of thine own being.

You can, however, apply this to everything. Wouldst thou heal man, look into the world on every side, see how on every side the world evolves processes of healing. Wouldst thou know the secrets of the world in the processes of illness and healing, look down into the depths of human nature. You can apply this to every aspect of man's being, but you must direct your gaze outwards to the great world of nature and see man in a living relationship with this great world.

People today have accustomed themselves to something different. They depart as far from nature as possible. They do something which shuts their own sight off from nature, for what they wish to examine they lay beneath a glass on a little stand—the eye does not look out into nature, but looks into the glass. Sight itself is cut off from nature. They call this a microscope. In certain connections it might as well be called a nulloscope, for it shuts one off from the great world of nature. People do not know, when something under the glass is magnified, that for spiritual knowledge it is exactly as though the same process were to take place in nature herself. For only think, when you take some minute particle from the human being for purposes of observation under a microscope, what you then do with this minute fragment is the same as if you were to stretch the man himself and tear him apart. You would be an even worse monster than Procrustes if you were to wrench man and tear him asunder in order to enlarge him as that minute particle is enlarged under the microscope. But do you believe that you would still have the person before you? This would naturally be out of the question. Just as little have you the reality there under the microscope. The truth which has been magnified is no longer the truth; it is an illusory image. We must not depart from nature and imprison our own sight. For other purposes, this can of course be useful; but for a true knowledge of man it is immensely misleading.

Knowledge of man in the true sense must be sought in the way we have indicated. Starting from the processes of nutrition, it must be followed through the processes of healing to the processes of human and world education in the widest sense. Or we can put it thus: from nutrition, through healing, to civilization and culture. For all that is concentrated in the nourishment of man is the groundwork, as it were, of his physical processes; the healing processes are derived from what continually encircles man, they are concentrated in the rhythmic system; and what comes from above is concentrated in man in the processes of the nerves and senses. Thus world-structure is erected on three levels.

This is what I wished to give you in the first place as a kind of foundation. We can now build further upon it. We shall see how, from such points of departure, we can actually progress to the business of practical affairs; and from thence we can lead over to a knowledge of the hierarchies.

LECTURE XI

10th November, 1923

You will have gathered from the foregoing descriptions that man's relation to his environment is very different from what modern ideas often conceive. It is so easy to think that what exists in man's surroundings, what belongs to the mineral, plant and animal kingdoms and is then taken into the body, that these external material processes which are investigated by the physicist, the chemist and so on, simply continue on in the same way within man himself. There can, however, be no question of this, for one must be clear that within the human skin-processes everything is different from outside it, that the world within differs entirely from the world without. As long as one is not aware of this one will ever and again reach the conclusion that what is examined in a retort, or investigated in some other way, is continued on inside the human organism, and the human organism itself will simply be regarded as a more complicated system of retorts.

You need only recall what I said in yesterday's lecture, that everything mineral within man must be transformed until it reaches the condition of warmth-ether. This means that everything of a mineral nature which enters into the human organism must be so far metamorphosed, so far changed, that at least for a certain period of time, it becomes pure warmth, becomes one with the warmth which man develops as his own individual temperature independent of the warmth of his environment. No matter whether it is salt or something else that we absorb, in one way or another it must assume the form of warmth-ether, and it must do this before it is made use of in the upbuilding of the living organism.

But something quite different is also connected with this : solid substance loses its solid form, when it is changed in the mouth into fluid, and is further transformed into the condition of warmth-ether. It loses weight when it gradually passes over into the fluid form, becomes more and more estranged from the earthly, but only when it has ascended to the warmth-etheric form is it fully prepared to absorb into itself the spiritual which comes from above, which comes from world-spaces.

Thus, if you would gain an idea of how a mineral substance functions in man, you must say the following : * There is the mineral substance; this mineral substance enters into man. Within man, passing through the fluid conditions, and so on, it is transformed into warmth-ether. Now it is warmth-ether. This warmth-ether has a strong disposition to absorb into itself what radiates inwards, what streams inwards, as forces from world-spaces. Thus it takes into itself the forces of the universe. And these forces of the universe now form themselves as the spiritual forces which here imbue the warmth-etherized earth-matter with spirit. And only then, with the help of the warmth-etherized earth-substance, does there enter into the body what the body needs for its formation.

So you see—if in the old sense we designate warmth as fire—we can say : What man absorbs in the way of mineral substance is carried upwards within him until it becomes of the nature of fire. And what is of the nature of fire has the disposition to take up into itself the influences of the higher hierarchies; and then this fire streams back again into all man's internal regions, and builds up, in that it re-solidifies, the material basis of the separate organs. Nothing that man takes into himself remains as it is; nothing remains earthly. Everything, for example, that comes from the mineral kingdom is so far transformed that it can take into itself the spiritual-cosmic, and only then, with the help of what comes from the spiritual cosmos, does it become re-solidified into the earthly condition.

Take from a bone, for instance, a fragment of calcium

* A diagram was drawn.

phosphate. This is in no way the calcium phosphate which you find outside in nature, or which, let us say, you introduce into the laboratory. It is the calcium phosphate which, while it arose from what was absorbed from outside, could only take part in building the human physical form, with the help of the forces which penetrated it during the time when it was changed into the warmth-ether condition.

This, you see, is why man needs substances of the most diverse kinds during the course of his life in order to be able, in accordance with the way he is organized at his particular age, to transform what is lifeless into the condition of warmth-ether. A child is as yet quite unable to change what is lifeless into the warmth-etheric condition; he has not enough strength in his organism. He must drink the milk which is still so nearly akin to the human organism in order to bring it into the condition of warmth-ether, and apply its forces to carrying out the full diffusion of plastic activity which is necessary during the years of childhood for the processes of bodily formation. One only gains insight into the nature of man when one knows that everything which is taken in from outside must be worked upon and basically transformed. Thus, if you take some external substance and wish to test its value for human life you simply cannot do this by means of ordinary chemistry. You must know how much force the human organism must exert in order to bring some external mineral substance, for example, to the fleeting condition of warmth-ether. If it is unable to do this, the external mineral substance is deposited, becoming heavy earth-matter before it has passed over into warmth, and penetrates into the human organism as inorganic matter which remains alien to human tissues.

An example of this kind can appear when the human being is not in a position to bring a substance, in its origin organic but appearing in him mineralized, namely sugar, to the tenuous condition of warmth-ether. Then arises the condition which must result when the whole organism has to share in the assimilation of what is thus present within it, the very serious condition of sugar diabetes. In the case of every ubstance one must therefore bear in mind to what degree he human organism can be in a position to transmute lifeless ubstance—whether its nature is already lifeless as when we at cooking salt, or whether it becomes so as with sugar—nto warmth-substance, whereby the organism which is rooted n the earth finds its union with the spiritual cosmos.

Every such deposit in man which remains untransmuted—as in diabetes—signifies that the human being does not find a union of the matter present within him and the spiritual of he cosmos. This is only a specific application of the general axiom that whatever approaches man from outside must be entirely worked over and transformed within him. And if we wish to look after a person's health it is of paramount importance to see to it that nothing enters into him which remains as it was, nothing which cannot be dealt with by the human organism until the least of its particles is transformed. This is not only the case in regard to substances; it is also the case, for instance, in regard to forces.

External warmth—the warmth we feel when we grasp things, the external warmth in the air—this, when taken up by the human organism, must become so transformed that he inner warmth is on a different level from the warmth outside. The external warmth must be transformed within us, so that this external warmth, in which we are not present, is laid hold of by the human organism even down to the very smallest quantity.

Now imagine that I go somewhere where it is cold, and because the cold is too intense, or, because of moving air or draught, the temperature fluctuates, I am not in a position to change the world warmth into my own individual warmth quickly enough. Through this I run the danger of being warmed by the world-warmth from outside like a piece of wood, or a stone. This should not be. I should not be exposed to the danger of external warmth flowing into me as though I were merely some object. At every moment, from the boundary of my skin inwards, I must be able to lay hold of the warmth and make it my own. If I am not in a position to do this I catch cold.

This is the inner process of catching cold. To catch cold is a poisoning by external warmth which is not taken possession of by the organism.

You see, everything in the external world is poison for man, actual poison, and it only becomes of service to him when, through his individual forces, he lays hold of it and makes it his own. For only from man himself do forces go up to the higher hierarchies in a human way; whereas outside man they remain with the elemental nature-beings, with the elemental spirits. In the case of man this wonderful transformation must happen so that within the human organism the elemental spirits may give over their work to the higher hierarchies. For the mineral in man this can only occur when it is absolutely and entirely transformed into warmth-ether.

Let us look at the plant world. Truly this plant world possesses something which bewitches man in the most varied way when he begins to contemplate the plant covering of the earth with the eye of the spirit. We go out into a meadow or a wood. We dig up, let us say, a plant with its root. If we regard what we have dug up with the eye of the spirit we find a wonderfully magical complex. The root shows itself as something of which we can say that it came into existence entirely in the sphere of the earthly. Yes, a plant root—the more so the coarser it appears—is really something terribly earthly. It always reminds one—especially a root like a turnip, for instance—of a particularly well-fed alderman. O, yes, it is so, the root of a plant is extremely smug, and self-satisfied. It has absorbed the salts of the earth into itself, and feels a deep sense of gratification at having soaked up the earth. In the whole sphere of the earthly there exists no more absolute expression of satisfaction than such a turnip-root; it is the representative of root-nature.

On the other hand let us look at the blossom. When we observe the blossom with the eye of the spirit we only experience it as our own soul, when it cherishes the tenderest desires

Only look at a spring flower; it is a sigh of longing, the embodiment of a wish. And something wonderful streams forth over the flower world which surrounds us, if only our soul-perception is delicate enough to be open to it. In spring we see the violet, maybe the daffodil, the lily-of-the-valley, or many little plants with yellow flowers, and we are seized by the feeling that these blossoming plants of spring would say to us: O Man, how pure and innocent can be the desires which you direct towards the spiritual! Spiritual desire-nature, desire-nature bathed, as it were, in piety, breathes from every blossom of spring.

And when the later flowers appear—let us at once take the other extreme, let us take the autumn crocus—can one behold the autumn crocus with soul-perception without having a slight feeling of shame? Does it not warn us that our desires can tend downwards, that our desires can be imbued with every kind of impurity? It is as though the autumn crocuses spoke to us from all sides, as if they would continually whisper to us: Consider the world of thy desires, O Man; how easily you can become a sinner!

Looked at thus, the plant-world is the mirror of human conscience in external nature. Nothing more poetical can be imagined than the thought of this voice of conscience coming forth from some point within us and being distributed over the myriad forms of the blossoming plants which speak to the soul, during the seasons of the year, in the most manifold ways. The plant-world reveals itself as the wide-spread mirror of conscience if we know how to look at it aright.

If we bear this in mind it becomes of special significance for us to look at the flowering plants and picture how the blossom is really a longing for the light-being of the universe, how the form of the blossom grows upwards in order to enable the desires of the earth to stream towards this light-being of the universe, and how on the other hand the substantial root fetters the plant to the earth, how it is the root which continually wrests the plant away from its celestial desires, wishing to re-establish it in the substantiality of the earth.

And we learn to understand why this is so when, in the evolutionary history of the earth, we meet the fact that what is present in the root of a plant has invariably been laid down in the time when the moon was still together with the earth.

In the time when the moon was still together with the earth the forces anchored in the moon within the body of the earth worked so strongly that they hardly allowed the plant to become anything but root. When the moon was still with the earth and the earth still had quite another substance, the root element spread itself out and worked downwards with great power. This can be pictured in such a way that one says : The downward thrust of the plant's root-nature spread out powerfully, while up above the plant only peeped out into the cosmos. We could say that the plants sent their shoots out into the cosmos like delicate little hairs. We feel that, while the moon was still with the earth, this moon element, these moon-forces, contained in the earth-body itself, fettered plant-nature to the earthly. And what was then transmitted to the being of the plant remains on as predisposition in the nature of the root.

After the moon left the earth, however, there unfolded in what had previously existed only as tiny little shoots peeping out into the world a longing for the wide light-filled spaces of the cosmos; and now the blossom-nature arose. So that the departure of the moon was a kind of liberation, a real liberation for the plants.

But here we must also bear in mind that everything earthly was grounded in the spiritual. During the old Saturn period—you need only take the description which I gave in my "Occult Science"—the earth was entirely spiritual; it existed only in the warmth-etheric element, it was entirely spiritual. It was out of the spiritual that the earthly was first formed.

And now let us contemplate the plant. In its form it bears the living memory of evolution. It bears in its root-nature the process of becoming earthly, of assuming the physical-material. If we look at the root of a plant we discern that it says something further to us, namely that its existence only became

possible because the earthly-material evolved out of the spiritual. Scarcely, however, was the earth relieved of its moon-
element than the plant again strove back to the spaces of the
light.

And when we consume the plant as nourishment we give
it the opportunity of carrying further in the right way what it
began outside in nature, the striving back not only to the
light-spaces, but to the spirit-spaces of the cosmos. This is
why, as I have already said, we must deal with the plant-
substance within us until it becomes aeriform, or gaseous, so
that the plant may follow its longing for the wide spaces of
light and spirit.

I go out into a meadow. I see how the flowers, the blossoms
of the plants, strive towards the light. Man consumes the
plant, but within him he has a world entirely different from
the one outside. Within him he can bring to fulfilment the
longing which, outside, the plant expresses in its blossoms.
Spread abroad in nature we see the desire-world of the plants.
We eat the plants. Within ourselves we drive this longing towards the spiritual world. We must therefore raise the plants
into the sphere of the air so that in this lighter realm they
may be enabled to strive towards the spiritual.

The plant here undergoes a remarkable process. When man
eats plant food the following occurs : If we depict the root
below,* and above what strives through the leaf to the
blossom, then, in this inner transference to the airy condition,
we have to experience a total reversal of the plant. The root,
which is fettered to the earth, just for the very reason that it
is so rooted, strives upwards; it strives upwards towards
the spiritual with such power that it leaves the striving of the
blossom behind it. It is actually as if you were to picture the
plant unfolding in such a way that the upper is pushed down
below and the lower up above. The plant reverses itself completely. The part which has already won its way to the blossom has had enjoyment in its material striving towards the
light, has brought the material up into the sphere of the light

* A diagram was drawn.

For this it must now suffer the punishment of remaining below. The root has been the slave of the earthly; but, as you can see from Goethe's theory of the metamorphosis of plants, it bears the whole plant-nature within it. It now strives upwards.

If a man is a really stiff-necked sinner, he is likely to remain so. But the root of a plant, which as long as it is earth-bound makes the impression of a well-fed alderman, immediately it has been eaten by man becomes transformed and strives upwards; whereas that which has brought the material into the sphere of the light, the blossom, must remain down below. Hence in what belongs to the root-element of the plant we have something which, when it is eaten, strives upwards towards man's head out of its inherent nature, while what lies in the direction of the blossom remains in the lower regions, and, in the general process of digestion, does not reach up to forming the head.

Thus we have the remarkable, the wonderful drama that when man consumes something of plant-nature—he need not eat the whole plant, because in each single part the whole plant is inherent (I refer you again to Goethe's theory of metamorphosis)—when man consumes a plant, it transforms itself within him into air, into air which develops plant-wise from above downwards, which grows and blossoms in a downward direction.

In times when such things were known through instinctive clairvoyance, people looked at the external constitution of plants in order to see whether they were such as could be beneficial to man's head, whether they showed a strong root-development, and in consequence a longing for the spiritual. For, when digestion is completed, what we have eaten of such a plant will seek out the head and penetrate it, so that it may there strive upwards towards the spiritual cosmos and enter into the necessary connection with it.

In the case of plants which are strongly imbued with astrality, for example, in the pod-bearing plants, their products remain in man's lower organism, and are unwilling to

ise up to the head, with the result that they produce a heavy
sleep, and dull the brain on waking. The Pythagoreans wished
to be clear thinkers and not introduce digestion into the functions of the head. This is why they forbade the eating of
beans.

You see, therefore, that from what happens in nature we
can divine something of nature's relation to man, and to what
happens in man. If one possesses spiritual initiation-science,
one simply cannot imagine how materialistic science comes to
grips with human digestion. (Certainly matters are different in
regard to a cow's digestion; about this, too, we shall have
something further to say later.) Materialistic science states
that plants are assimilated just as they are. They are not
assimilated just as they are, but are completely spiritualized. The plant is so constituted in itself that in digestion the
lower turns into the upper and the upper into the lower. No
greater transposition can be imagined. And man immediately
becomes ill if he eats even the smallest quantity of a plant
where the lowest is not changed into the uppermost, and the
uppermost into the lowest.

From this you will realize that man bears nothing in himself
which is not produced by the spirit; he must first give to what
he assimilates as substance a form which will enable the spirit
to influence it.

Turning now to the animal world, we must be clear that
the animal has a digestion, and mostly consumes plants. Let
us take the herbivorous animal. The animal world takes the
plant world into itself. This again is a very complicated process, for when the animal eats the plant it does not possess
human processes to set against the plant. Within the animal
the plant cannot turn the above into the below and the below
into the above. The animal has its vertebral column parallel
with the surface of the earth. This means that in the case of
the animal what should happen in digestion is brought into
complete disorder. What is below strives upwards, and what
is above strives downwards, but the whole process gets dam-
med up in itself, so that animal digestion is something

essentially different from human digestion. In animal digestion, what lives in the plant dams itself up. And the result of
this is that with the animal the being of the plant is given the
promise: "Thou mayest indulge thy longing for world-spaces"
—but the promise is not kept. The plant is thrown back again
to earth.

Through the fact, however, that in the animal organism the
plant is thrown back to earth, there immediately penetrate
into the plant—not, as with man in whom the reversal takes
place, cosmic spirits with their forces, but certain elemental
spirits in their place. And these elemental spirits are fear-
spirits, bearers of fear. Thus spiritual perception can follow this
remarkable process: The animal itself enjoys its nourishment,
enjoys it with inner satisfaction; and while the stream of
nourishment goes in one direction, a stream of fear from
elemental spirits of fear goes in the other. Through the
animal's digestive tract there continually flows along the path
of digestion the satisfaction felt in the assimilation of nourishment, and in opposition to this there flows a terrible stream
of elemental spirits of fear.

This is what animals leave behind them when they die.
When animals die—not those species, perhaps, which I have
already described in another way, but including such as belong, for instance, to the four-footed mammals—when these
animals die there also dies, or rather comes to life in their
dying, a being which is entirely composed of the element of
fear. With the animal's death, fear dies, that is to say fear
comes to life. In the case of beasts of prey this fear is actually
assimilated with their food. The beast of prey, which tears its
booty to pieces, devours the flesh with satisfaction. And towards this satisfaction in the consumption of flesh there
streams fear, the fear which the plant-eating animal only gives
off from itself when it dies, but which already streams out from
the beast of prey during its life-time. Through this the astral
bodies of such animals as lions and tigers are riddled with
fear which they do not as yet detect during their lifetime, but
which after death these animals drive back because it goes in

opposition to their feeling of satisfaction. Thus carnivorous animals really have an after life in their group soul, an after life which must be said to present a much more terrible Kamaloka than anything which can be experienced by man, and this simply on account of their essential nature.

Naturally you must regard these things as being experienced in quite a different consciousness. If you were suddenly to become materialistic, and began to imagine what the beast of prey must experience by putting yourself in its place, thinking : What would such a Kamaloka be like for me? and were then to judge the beast of prey according to what such a Kamaloka might be for *you*, then certainly you are materialistic, indeed animalistic, for you transpose yourself into animal nature. These things must of course be understood if one is to comprehend the world; but we must not put ourselves into their category, as when the materialistic puts the whole world into the category of lifeless matter.

Now we come to a subject about which I can only speak on a soul level; for anthroposophy should never come forward to agitate for anything, should never advocate either one thing or another, but should only put forward the truth. The consequences which a person attracts to himself by his manner of living, this is his personal affair. Anthroposophy presents no dogmas, but puts forward truths. For this reason I shall never, even for fanatics, lay down any kind of law as to the consequences of what an animal makes of its plant nourishment. No dogmatic rulings shall be given in regard to vegetarianism, meat-eating and so on, for these things must be relegated to the sphere of individual judgment and it is really only in the sphere of individual experience that they have value. I mention this in order to avoid giving rise to the opinion that anthroposophy entails standing for this or that kind of diet, whereas what it actually does is to make every diet comprehensible.

What I really wished to say was that we must work upon the mineral until it becomes warmth-ether in order that it may absorb the spiritual; then, after the mineral has absorbed the spiritual, man can be built up by it. I mentioned that when the human being is still quite young he has not as yet the strength to work upon what is entirely mineral until it becomes warmth-ether. It has already been worked upon for him in that he drinks milk. Milk has already undergone a preliminary change, whereby the process of transformation to warmth-ether has become easier. Hence in a child the milk with its forces flows up quickly into the head, and can there develop the form-building forces in the way in which the child needs them. For the whole organization of the child proceeds from the head.

If at a later age man wishes to receive these form-building forces, it is not good to promote them by the drinking of milk. In the case of the child what ascends into the head, and is able by means of the forces of the head, which are present until the change of teeth, to ray out formatively into the whole body—this is no longer present in an older person. In later age the whole of the rest of the organism must ray out the formative forces. And these formative forces for the whole organism are particularly strengthened in their impulses when one eats something which works in quite another way than is the case with the head.

You see, the head is entirely enclosed. Within this head are the impulses used in childhood for the formation of the body. In the rest of the body we have bones within, and the formative forces outside. Here, then, the form-building forces must be stimulated from outside. While we are children these form-building forces are stimulated when we bring milk into the head. When we are no longer children these forces are no longer there. What should we now do in order that these formative forces may be stimulated more from outside?

It would obviously be a good thing to be able to have in outer form what is accomplished within by the head, enclosed as it is inside skull. It would be good if what the head does inside itself could somehow be accomplished in outer form from outside. The forces which are there within the head are suited to the consumption of milk; when the milk is there in

its etheric transformation it provides a good basis for the
development of these head forces. We must, therefore, have
something which acts like milk, which, however, is not fabricated within the human being, but is fabricated in outer
nature.

Well, there is something existing outside in nature which is
a head without an enclosing skull, and which therefore acti-
vates from outside those very forces which work inside the
head in children who need the milk, and must indeed create
it anew; for the child must first bring the milk into the
warmth-etheric condition and so create it anew.

Now a stock of bees is really a head which is open on all
sides. What the bees carry out is actually the same as what
the head carries out within itself. The hive we give them is at
most a support. The bees activity, however, is not enclosed,
but produced from outside. In a stock of bees, under external
spiritual influence, we have the same thing as we have under
spiritual influence inside the head. The stock of bees produces
its honey, and when we eat and enjoy honey it gives us the
upbuilding forces, which must now be provided more from
outside, with the same strength and power which milk gives
us for our head during the years of childhood.

Thus, while we are still children we strengthen through the
consumption of milk the formative forces working from the
head outwards; if at a later age we still need formative forces
we must eat honey. Nor do we need to eat it in tremendous
quantities—it is only a question of absorbing its forces.

Thus one learns from external nature how strengthening
forces must be brought into human life, if only this external
nature is fully understood. And if we would conceive a land
where there are beautiful children and beautiful old people,
what kind of a land would this be? It would be "a land flowing with milk and honey". So you see ancient instinctive
vision was in no way wrong when it said about lands of
promise that they are such as flow with milk and honey.

Many such simple sayings contain the profoundest wisdom,
and there is really no more beautiful experience than first to

make every possible effort to experience the truth, and then to find some ancient holy saying abounding in deep wisdom such as "a land flowing with milk and honey". That is indeed a rare land, for in it there are only beautiful children and beautiful old people.

You see, to understand man presupposes the understanding of nature. To understand nature provides the basis for the understanding of man. And here the lowest spheres of the material always lead up to the highest spheres of the spiritual : the kingdoms of nature—mineral, animal, vegetable—at the one, the lowest pole; above, at the other pole, the hierarchies themselves.

LECTURE XII

11th November, 1923

When we realize that everything of external nature is transformed inside the human organism, and this in so radical a way that the mineral must be brought to the warmth-etheric condition, we will also find that all that lives in man, in the human organization, flows out into the spiritual. If—according to the ideas so frequently deduced in current text-books on anatomy and physiology—we imagine man to be a firmly built form taking into itself the products of external nature and returning them almost unchanged, then we will always labour under the absence of the bridge which must be thrown from what man is as a natural being to what is present in him as his essential soul-nature.

At first we shall be unable to find any link to join the bony system and system of muscles, composing the solid body which man believes himself to be, with, let us say, the moral world-order. It will be said that the one is simply nature and that the other is something radically different from nature. But when we are clear about the fact that in man all types of substantiality are present and that they must all pass through a condition more volatile than that of muscles and bones, we shall find that this volatile etheric substance can enter into connection with the impulses of the moral world-order.

These are the modes of thought we must use if we are to develop our present considerations into something which will lead man upwards to the spiritual of the cosmos, to the beings whom we have called the beings of the higher hierarchies. Today, therefore, let us do what was not done in the foregoing lectures—for those were more occupied with the natural world—and take our start from the spiritual moral impulses active in man.

The spiritual-moral impulses—well, for modern civilization these have more or less become mere abstract concepts. To an ever greater degree the primal feeling for the moral-spiritual has receded in human nature. Through the whole manner of his education modern civilization leads man to ask: what is customary? what has convention ordained? what is the code? what is the law?—and so on. Less account is taken of what comes forth as impulses, rooted in that part of man which is often relegated in a vague way to conscience. This inner directing of oneself, this determining of one's own goal, is something which has retreated to an ever greater degree in modern civilization. Hence the spiritual-moral has finally become a more or less conventional tradition.

Earlier world-conceptions, particularly those which were sustained by instinctive clairvoyance, brought forth moral impulses from man's inner nature; they induced moral impulses. Moral impulses exist, but today they have become traditional. Of course nothing whatever is implied here against the traditional in morality—but only think of the ten commandments, how old they are. They are taught as commands recorded in ancient times. Is it to be expected today that something might spring forth from the primary, elementary sources of human nature which could be compared to what once arose as the Decalogue, the Ten Commandments? Now from what source does the moral-spiritual arise, which binds men together in a social way, which knits the threads uniting man to man? There exists only one true source of the moral-spiritual in mankind, and this is what we may call human understanding, mutual human understanding, and, based upon this human understanding, human love. Wheresoever we may look for the arising of moral-spiritual impulses in mankind, in so far as these play a role in social life, it will invariably prove to be the case that, whenever such impulses spring forth with elemental power, they arise from human understanding based upon human love. These are the actual driving force of the social moral-spiritual impulses in mankind. And fundamentally speaking, in so far as he is a spiritual being, man only lives with other men to the degree that he develops human understanding and human love.

Here one can put a deeply significant question, a question which is indeed not always voiced, but which, in regard to what has just been said, must be on the tip of every tongue: If human understanding and human love are the real impulses upon which communal life depends, how does it come about that the very reverse of human understanding and human love appears in our social order?

This is a question with which initiates more than anyone else have always concerned themselves. In every age in which initiation science was the primal impulse, this very question was regarded as one of their most vital concerns. When this initiation science was still a primary impulse, however, it possessed certain means whereby to get behind this problem. But if one looks at conventional science today, one is forced to ask: As the god-created soul is naturally predisposed to human understanding and human love, why are these qualities not active as a matter of course in the social order? Whence come human hatred and lack of human understanding? Now, if we are unable to look for this lack of human understanding, this human hatred, in the sphere of the spiritual, of the soul, it follows that we must look for them in the sphere of the physical.

Yes—but now modern conventional science gives us its answer as to what the physical-bodily nature of man is: blood, nerves, muscles, bones. No matter how long one studies a bone, if one only does so with the eye of present-day natural science, one will never be able to say: It is this bone which leads man astray into hatred. Nor yet, to whatever degree one is able to investigate the blood according to the principles by which it is investigated today, will one ever be able to establish the conviction: It is this blood which leads man astray into lack of human understanding.

In times when initiation science was a primal impulse

matters were certainly quite otherwise. Then one turned one's gaze to the physical-bodily nature of man and perceived it to be the counter-image of what one possessed of the spiritual through instinctive clairvoyance.

When man speaks of the spiritual today he refers at most to abstract thoughts; this for him is the spiritual. If he finds these thoughts too tenuous, all that remains to him is words, and then, as Fritz Mauthner did, he writes a "Critique of Language". Through such a "Critique of Language" he manages to dilute the spirit—already tenuous enough—until it becomes utterly devoid of substance. The initiation-science which was irradiated with instinctive clairvoyance did not see the spiritual in abstract thoughts. It saw the spiritual in forms, in what produced pictures, in what could speak and resound, in what could produce tones. For this initiation science the spiritual lived and moved. And because the spiritual was seen in its living activity, what is physical—the bones, the blood—could also be perceived in its spirituality. These thoughts, these notions, which we have today about the skeleton, did not exist in initiation science. Today the skeleton is really regarded as something constructed by the calculations of an architect for the purposes of physiology and anatomy. But it is not this. The skeleton, as you have seen, is formed by mineral substance which has been driven upwards to the state of warmth-ether, so that in the warmth-ether the forces of the higher hierarchies are laid hold of, and then the bone-formations are built up.

To one who is able to behold it rightly, the skeleton reveals its spiritual origin. But one who looks at the skeleton in its present form—I mean in its form as present-day science regards it—is like a person who says: there I have a printed page with the forms of letters upon it. He describes the form of these letters, but does not read their meaning because he is unable to read. He does not relate what is expressed in the forms of the letters to what exists as their real basis; he only describes their shapes. In the same way the present-day anatomist, the present-day natural scientist, describes the bones as if they were entirely without meaning. What they really reveal, however, is their origin in the spiritual.

And so it is with everything that exists as physical natural laws, as etheric natural laws. They are written characters from the spiritual world. And we only understand these things rightly when we can comprehend them as written characters proceeding from spiritual worlds.

Now, when we are able to regard the human organism in this way, we become aware of something which belongs to the domain of which the true initiates of all epochs have said : When one crosses the threshold into the spiritual world, the first thing one becomes aware of is something terrible, something which at first it is by no means easy to sustain. Most people wish to be pleasantly affected by what seems to them worthy of attainment. But the fact remains that only by passing through the experience of horror can one learn to know spiritual reality, that is to say true reality. For in regard to the human form, as this is placed before us by anatomy and physiology, one can only perceive that it is built up out of two elements from the spiritual world : moral coldness and hatred.

In our souls we actually possess the predisposition to human love, and to that warmth which understands the other man. In the solid components of our organism, however, we bear moral cold. This is the force which, from the spiritual worlds, welds, as it were, our physical organism together. Thus we bear in ourselves the impulse of hatred. This it is which, from the spiritual world, brings about the circulation of the blood. And whereas we may perhaps go through the world with a very loving soul, with a soul which thirsts for human understanding, we must nevertheless be aware that below in the unconsciousness, there where the soul streams down, sends its impulses down into the bodily nature, for the very purpose that we may be clothed in a body—coldness has its seat. Though I shall always speak just of coldness, what I mean is moral coldness, though this can certainly pass over into physical coldness, traversing the warmth-ether on its way. There below, in the unconsciousness within us, moral coldness and hatred are entrenched, and it is easy for man to bring into his soul what is present in his body, so that his soul can, as it were, be infected with the lack of human understanding. This is, however, the result of moral coldness and human hatred. Because this is so, man must gradually cultivate in himself moral warmth, that is to say human understanding and love, for these must vanquish what comes from the bodily nature.

Now it cannot be denied—this presents itself in all clarity to spiritual vision—that in our age, which began with the fifteenth century and has developed in an intellectualistic way on the one hand and in a materialistic way on the other, much human misunderstanding and human hatred has become imbedded in men's souls. This is so to a greater degree than is supposed. For only when man passes through the gate of death does he become aware of how much failure to understand, how much hatred, is present in our unconsciousness. There man detaches his soul-spiritual from his physical-bodily nature. He lays his physical-bodily nature aside. The impulses of coldness, the impulses of hatred, then reveal themselves simply as natural forces, as mere forces of nature.

Let us look at a corpse. Let us look with the spiritual eye at the actual etheric corpse. Here we are looking at something which no longer evokes moral judgment any more than does a plant or a stone. The moral forces which have previously been contained in what is now the corpse have been changed into natural forces. During his lifetime, however, the human being absorbed very much from them; this he takes with him through the gate of death. The ego and astral body withdraw, taking with them as they go what remained unnoticed during life because it was always entirely submerged in the physical and etheric bodies. The ego and astral body take with them into the spiritual world all the impulses connected with the human body, all the impulses of human hatred and coldness towards other men which had gained access to their souls. I mentioned that it is only when one sees the human being pass through the gate of death that one perceives how much failure to understand, how much human hatred have been implanted into mankind just in our civilization by various things about which I shall still have to speak. For the man of today carries much of these two impulses through the gate of death, immensely much.

But what man thus carries with him is in fact the spiritual residue of what should be in the physical, of what the physical and etheric bodies should deal with themselves. In the lack of human understanding and in human hatred which man carries into the spiritual world we have the residue of what really belongs in the physical world. He carries it thither in a spiritual way, but it would never profit him to carry it onward through the time between death and a new birth, for then he would be quite unable to progress. At every step in his further evolution between death and a new birth he would stumble if he were obliged to carry further this failure to understand the other man, this human hatred. Into the spiritual world, which is entered by the so-called dead, people today continually draw with them definite currents which would halt them in their development if they had to remain as they actually are. From whence do these currents proceed?

To discover this we need only look at present-day life. People pass one another by; they pay little heed to the individual characteristics of others. Are not people today mostly so constituted that each one regards himself as the standard of what is right and proper? And when someone differs from this standard we do not take kindly to him, but rather think: This man should be different. And this usually implies: He should be like me. This is not always brought into the consciousness, but it lies concealed in human social intercourse.

In the way things are put forward today—I mean in the whole manner and form of people's speech—there lies very little understanding of the other man. People bellow out their ideas about what man should be like, but this usually means: Everyone should be like me. If someone different comes along, then, even if this is not consciously realized, he is immediately regarded as an enemy, an object for antipathy. This is lack of human moral understanding, lack of love. And to the degree in which these qualities are lacking, moral coldness and human hatred go with man through the gate of death, obstructing his path. Now, however—because man's further development is not his own concern alone, but is the concern of the whole world-order, the wisdom-filled world-order—he finds the beings of the third hierarchy, Angels, Archangels, Archai. In the first period after man has passed through the gate of death into the world lying between death and a new birth these beings stoop downward and mercifully take from man the coldness which comes from lack of human understanding. And we see how the beings of the third hierarchy assume the burden of what man carries up to them into the spiritual world in the way I have described, in that he passes through the gate of death.

It is for a longer period that man must carry with him the remains of human hatred; for this can only be taken from him by grace of the spirits of the second hierarchy, Exusiai, Kyriotetes, Dynamis. They take from him all that remains of human hatred.

Now, however, the human being has arrived about midway in the region between death and a new birth, to the abiding place of the first hierarchy, Seraphim, Cherubim, Thrones, which I described in my Mystery Play as the midnight hour of existence. Man would be quite unable to pass through this region of the Seraphim, Cherubim, and Thrones without being inwardly annihilated, utterly destroyed, had not the beings of the second and third hierarchies already taken from him in their mercy human misunderstanding, that is to say moral coldness, and human hatred. And so we see how man, in order that he may find access to those impulses which can contribute to his further development, must at first burden the beings of the higher hierarchies with what he carries up into the spiritual world from his physical and etheric bodies, where it really belongs.

When one has insight into all this, when one sees how this

moral coldness holds sway in the spiritual world, one will also know how to judge the relation between this spiritual cold and the physical cold here below. The physical cold which we find in snow and ice is only the physical image of that moral-spiritual cold which is there above. If we have them both before us, we can compare them. While man is being relieved in this way from human misunderstanding and human hatred, one can follow with the spiritual eye how he begins to lose his form, how this form more or less melts away.

When someone first passes through the gate of death, for the spiritual vision of imagination his appearance is still somewhat similar to what it was here on earth. For what a man bears within him here on earth is in fact just substances in more or less granular form, let us say, in atomistic form; but the human figure itself—that is spiritual. We must really be clear about this. It is sheer nonsense to regard man's form as physical; we must represent it to ourselves as spiritual. The physical in it is everywhere present as minute particles. The form, which is only a force-body, holds together what would otherwise fall apart into a heap of atoms. If someone were to take any of you by the forelock and could draw out your form, the physical and also the etheric would collapse like a heap of sand. That these are not just a sandheap, that they are distributed and take on form, this stems from nothing physical; it stems from the spiritual. Here in the physical world man goes about as something spiritual. It is senseless to think that man is only a physical being; his form is purely spiritual. The physical in him may almost be likened to a heap of crumbs.

Man, however, still possesses his form when he goes through the gate of death. One sees it shimmering, glittering, radiant with colours. But now he loses first the form of his head; then the rest of his form gradually melts away. Man becomes completely metamorphosed, as though transformed into an image of the cosmos. This occurs during the time between death and a new birth in which he comes into the region of the Seraphim, Cherubim and Thrones.

Thus, when one follows man between death and a new birth, one at first still sees him hovering, as it were, while he gradually loses his form from above downwards. But while the last vestige of him is vanishing away below, something else has taken shape, a wonderful spirit-form, which is in itself an image of the whole world-sphere and at the same time a model of the future head which man will bear on his shoulders. Here the human being is woven into an activity wherein not only the beings of the lower hierarchies participate, but also the beings of the highest hierarchy, the Seraphim, Cherubim and Thrones.

What actually takes place? It is the most wonderful thing which, as man, one can possibly conceive. For all that was lower man here in life now passes over into the formation of the future head. As we go about here on earth we only make use of our poverty-stricken head as the organ of our mental images and our thoughts. But thoughts also accompany our breast, thoughts also accompany our limb-system. And in the moment that we cease to think only with the head, but begin to think with our limb-system, in that moment the whole reality of Karma is opened up to us. We know nothing of our Karma because we always think only with that most superficial of organs, our brain. The moment we begin to think with our fingers—and just with our fingers and toes we can think much more clearly than with the nerves of the head —once we have soared up to the possibility of doing so—the moment we begin to think with what has not become entirely material, when we begin to think with the lower man, our thoughts are the thoughts of our Karma. When we do not merely grasp with our hand but think with it, then, thinking with our hand we follow our Karma. And even more so with the feet; when we do not only walk but think with our feet, we follow the course of our Karma with special clarity. That man is such a dullard on earth—excuse me, but no other word occurs to me—comes from the fact that all his thinking is enclosed in the region of his head. But man can think with his entire being. Whenever we think with our entire being, then for our middle region a whole cosmology, a marvellous cosmic wisdom, becomes our own. And for the lower region and the limb-system especially Karma becomes our own.

It already means a great deal when we look at the way a person walks, not in a dull way, but marking the beauty of his step, and what is characteristic in it; or when we allow his hands to make an impression upon us, so that we interpret these hands and find that in every movement of the fingers there lie wonderful revelations of man's inner nature. Yet that is only the smallest part of what moves in unison with the walking man, the grasping man, man as he moves his fingers. For it is man's whole moral nature which moves; his destiny moves with him; everything that he is as a spiritual being. And if, after man has passed through the gate of death, we are able to follow how his form dissolves—the first to melt away being what is reminiscent of his physical form—there then appears what does indeed resemble his physical structure, but which is now produced by his inner nature, his inner being, thus announcing that this is his moral form. Thus does man appear when he approaches the midnight hour of exist- ence, when he comes into the sphere of the Seraphim, Cheru- bim and Thrones. Then we see how these wonderful meta- morphoses proceed, how there his form melts away. But this is not really the essential point. It looks as though the form would dissolve away, but the truth is that the spiritual beings of the higher worlds are there working together with man. They work with those human beings who are working upon themselves, but also upon those with whom they are karmic- ally linked. One man works upon the other. These spiritual beings, then, together with man himself, develop out of his previous bodily form in his previous earth-life, what, at first spiritually, will become the bodily form of his next earth-life.

This spirit-form first connects itself with physical life when it meets the given embryo. But in the spiritual world feet and legs are transformed into the jaw bones, while arms and hands are transformed into the cheek-bones. There the whole lower man is transformed into the spiritual prototype of what will later become the head. The way in which this metamorphosis is accomplished is, I do assure you, of everything that the world offers to conscious experience the most wonderful. We see at first how an image of the whole cosmos is created, and how this is then differentiated into the structure which is the seat of the whole moral element—but only after all that I have mentioned has been taken from it. We see how what was transforms itself into what will be. Now one sees the human being as spirit-form journeying back once more to the region of the second hierarchy and then to that of the third hierarchy. Here this reversed spirit-form—it is in fact only the basis for the future head—must, as it were, be welded to what will become the future breast-organism, to what will become the future limb-organization and the metabolic system. These must be added. Whence come the spiritual impulses to add them?

It is by grace of the beings of the second and third hierarchies, who gathered these impulses together when the man was on the first half of his journey. These beings took them from his moral nature; now they bring them back again and form from them the basis of the rhythmic system and meta-bolic-limb-system. In this later period between death and a new birth man receives the ingredients, the spiritual ingredients, for his physical organism. This spiritual form finds its way into the embryonic life, and bears within it what will now become physical forces and etheric forces. These are, however, only the physical image of what we bear in us from our previous life as lack of human understanding and human hatred, from which our limb-organization is spiritually formed.

If we wish to have such conceptions as these, we must acquire a manner of feeling and perceiving quite other than that needed in the physical world. For we must be able to behold what arises out of the spiritual becoming physical in the way I have described; we must be able to sustain the knowledge that coldness, moral coldness, lives as physical image in the bones and that moral hatred lives as physical image in

the blood. We must learn to look at these matters quite objectively. It is only when we look into things in this way that
we become aware of the fundamental difference between
man's inner being and external nature.

Just consider for a moment the fact I mentioned, namely
that in the blossoms of the plant-kingdom we see, as it were,
human conscience laid out before us. What we see outside
us may be considered as the picture of our soul-being. The
forces within ourselves may appear to have no relation to outer
nature. But the truth is, bone can only be bone because it
hates the carbonic acid and calcium phosphate in their mineral
state, because it withdraws from them, contracting into itself,
whereby it becomes something different from what these substances are in external nature. And one must face up to the
conception that for man to have a physical form, hatred and
coldness must be present in his physical nature.

Through this, you see, our words gain inner significance. If
our bones have a certain hardness, it is to their advantage to
possess this physical image of spiritual coldness. But if our
soul has this hardness it is not a good thing for the social life.
The physical nature of man must be different from his soul-
nature. Man can be man precisely because his physical being
differs from his being of soul and spirit. Man's physical nature
also differs from physical nature around him. Upon this fact
rests the necessity for that transformation about which I have
spoken to you.

All this forms an important supplement to what I once
said in the course on Cosmology, Philosophy and Religion*
about man's connection with the hierarchies. It could only
be added, however, on such initial considerations as those
in our present lectures. For spiritual vision gives insight alike
into what the separate members of the mineral, animal and
plant kingdoms really are here on earth, and into the acts of
the hierarchies—those acts, which continue from age to age,
as do also the happenings of nature and the works of man.

* Ten lectures at the Goetheanum, September, 1922. Translation
in preparation by the Anthroposophic Press, New York.

When man's life between death and a new birth—his life in the spiritual world—is beheld in this way, one can describe his experiences in that world in just as much detail as his biography here on earth. So we may live in the hope that when we pass through the gate of death, everything of misunderstanding and hatred between man and man will be carried up into the spiritual world, so that it may be given anew to us, and that from its ennobled state human forms may be created.

In the course of long centuries something very strange has come to pass for earthly humanity. No longer is it possible for all the forces of human misunderstanding and human hatred to be used up in new human forms, in the structure of new human bodies. Something has become left over. During the course of the last centuries this residue has streamed down on to the earth, so that in the spiritual atmosphere of the earth, in what I may call the earth's astral light, there is to be found an infiltration of the impulses of human hatred and human misunderstanding which exist exterior to man. These impulses have not been incorporated into human forms; they stream around the earth in the astral light. They work into man, but not into what makes up the single person but into the relationships which people form with one another on the earth. They work into civilization. And within civilization they have brought about what compelled me to say, in the spring of 1914 in Vienna,* that our present-day civilization is invaded by spiritual carcinoma, by a spiritual cancerous disease, by spiritual tumours. At that time the fact that this was spoken about in Vienna—in the lecture-course dealing with the phenomena between death and a new birth—was somewhat unwelcome. Since then, however, people have actually experienced something of the truth of what was said at that time. Then people had no thought of what streams through civilization. They did not perceive that actual cancerous formations of civilization were present, for it was only

* *The Inner Nature of Man and Life between Death and Rebirth* (Rudolf Steiner Press).

from 1914 onwards that they manifested openly. Today they
are revealed as utterly diseased tissues of civilization. Yes, now
it becomes evident to what a degree our modern civilization
has been infiltrated by these currents of human hatred and
human coldness which have not been used up in the forms
of the human structure, to what a degree these infiltrations
are active as the parasites of modern civilization.

Civilization today is deeply afflicted with parasites; it is
like a part of an organism that is invaded by parasites, by
bacilli. What people have amassed in the way of thoughts
exists, but it has no living connection with man. Only consider how this shows itself in the most ordinary phenomena
of daily life. How many people have to learn without bringing
enthusiasm to the learning; they simply have to get down to it
and learn in order to pass an examination, so as to qualify
for some particular post, or the like—well, for them there is
no vital connection between what they have to take in and
what lives in their soul as an inborn craving for the spiritual.
It is exactly as though a person who is not predisposed to
hunger were to be continually stuffed with food! The digestive processes about which I have spoken cannot be carried
through. What has been taken in remains as ballast in the
organism, finally becoming something which definitely induces
parasites.

Much in our modern civilization has no connection with
man. Like the mistletoe—spiritually speaking—it sucks its life
from what man brings forth from the original impulses of his
mind, of his heart. Much of this manifests in our civilization
as parasitic existence. To anyone who has the power of
seeing our civilization with spiritual vision in the astral, the
year 1914 already presented an advanced stage of cancer, a
carcinoma formation; for him the whole of civilization was
already invaded by parasites. But to this parasitic condition
something further is now added.

I have described to you in what may be called a spiritual-
physiological way how, out of the nature of the gnomes and
undines who work from below upwards, the possibility arises

of parasitic impulses in man. Then, however, as I explained, the opposite picture presents itself; for then poison is carried downwards by the sylphs and the elemental beings of warmth. And so in a civilization like ours, which bears a parasitic character, what comes down from above—spiritual truth, though not poison in itself, is transformed into poison in man, so that our civilization rejects it in fear and invents all kinds of reasons for this rejection. The two things belong together : a parasitic culture below, which does not proceed from elemental laws and which therefore contains parasites within itself, and a spirituality which sinks down from above and which—in that it enters into this civilization—is taken up by man in such a way that it becomes poison. When you bear this in mind you have the key to the most important symptoms of our present-day civilization. And when one has insight into these things, just out of itself the fact is revealed that a truly cultural education must make its appearance as the antidote or opposing remedy. Just as a rational therapy is deduced from a true diagnosis of the individual, so a diagnosis of the sickness of a civilization reveals the remedy; the one calls forth the other.

It is very evident that mankind today again needs something from civilization which stands close to the human heart and the human soul, which springs directly from the human heart and the human soul. If a child, on entering primary school, is introduced to a highly sophisticated system of letter-forms which he has to learn as a . . . b . . . c etc., this has nothing whatever to do with his heart and soul. It has no relation to them at all. What the child develops in his head, in his soul, in that he has to learn a . . . b . . . c, is—speaking spiritually— a parasite in human nature.

During his years of education a great deal is brought to the child of this parasitic nature. We must, therefore, develop an art of education which works creatively from his soul. We must let the child bring colour into form; and the colour-forms, which have arisen out of joy, out of enthusiasm, out of sadness, out of every possible feeling, these he can paint

on to the paper. When a child puts on to the paper what
arises out of his soul, this develops his humanity. This produces
nothing parasitic. This is something which grows out of man
like his fingers or his nose!—whereas, when the child has
forced on him the conventional forms of the letters, which
are the result of a high degree of civilization, this does
engender what is parasitic.

Immediately the art of education lies close to the human
heart, to the human soul, the spiritual approaches man without becoming poison. First you have the diagnosis, which finds
that our age is infested with carcinomas, and then you have
the therapy—yes, it is Waldorf School education.

Waldorf School education is founded upon nothing other
than this, my dear friends. Its way of thinking in the cultural
sphere is the same as that in the field of therapy. Here you see,
applied in a special case, what I spoke about a few days ago,
namely that the being of man proceeds from below upwards,
from nutrition, through healing, upwards to the development
of the spiritual, and that one must regard education as medicine transposed into the spiritual. This strikes us with particular clarity when we wish to find a therapy for civilization, for
we can only conceive this therapy as being Waldorf School
education.

You will readily be able to imagine the feelings of one who
not only has insight into this situation, but who is also trying
to implant Waldorf School education into the world in a
practical way, when he sees in the cumulative effect of this
carcinoma of civilization something which may seriously en-
danger this Waldorf School education, or even make it alto-
gether impossible. We should not reject such thoughts as these,
but rather make them the impulse within ourselves to
work together wherever we still can in the therapy of our
civilization.

There are many things today such as the following. During
my Helsingfors lecture-course in 1913, I indicated from a
certain aspect of spiritual knowledge a view as to the inferior
nature of Woodrow Wilson, who was at that time a veritable

object of veneration for much of civilized mankind and in respect of whom people are only now—because to do otherwise is impossible—gaining some measure of perception. As things went then, so have things also gone in regard to the civilization-carcinoma about which I have been speaking. Well, at that time things went in a certain way; today those things which hold good for our time are proceeding in a similar manner. People are asleep. It devolves upon us to bring about the awakening. And Anthroposophy bears within it all the impulses for a right awakening of civilization, for a right awakening of human culture.

This is what I wished to say to you in the last of these lectures.

Books for further reading:

By RUDOLF STEINER

The Study of Man
Man in the Light of Occultism
Macrocosm and Microcosm
Supersensible Man
Spiritual Hierarchies
The Influence of Spiritual Beings upon Man
The Effects of Spiritual Development
Theosophy – An Introduction

By HERMANN POPPELBAUM

Man and Animal
A New Zoology

By WOLFGANG SCHAD

Man and Mammals

By GERBERT GROHMANN

The Plant

By STEWART EASTON

Man and the World in the Light of Anthroposophy